MIKE POWER'S

PUB WALKS

IN

HARDY'S WESSEX

Biographical notes, literary associations and historical interest by Brenda Flint.

1st edition published Nov 97

© Power Publications
ISBN 1 898073 14 7

Publishers note
Whilst every care has been taken to ensure that all the information contained in this book is correct neither the authors or publishers can accept any responsibility for any inaccuracies that occur.

Other pub walking books
'Pub Walks in The New Forest'
'Pub Walks in Dorset'
'Forty More Pub Walks in Dorset'
'Pub Walks in Hampshire and the I.O.W.'
'Pub Walks in Devon'
'Pub Walks in Cornwall'
'Pub Walks in West Sussex'
'Pub Walks in East Sussex'
'Pub Walks in Kent'
'Pub Walks in Somerset' (1998)

Power Publications
1 Clayford Ave
Ferndown
DORSET. BH22 9PQ

Printed by Pardy & Son (Printers) Ltd., Ringwood, Hampshire
Cover photograph: Mike Power

INTRODUCTION

Whilst writing the Dorset books in our very successful pub walking series the name of Thomas Hardy occurred again and again and gave me the idea for a new and original guide based solely on 'Hardy's Wessex'.

Thomas Hardy was born in the family cottage at Higher Bockhampton in the parish of Stinsford, near Dorchester, on 2 June 1840. This part of Dorset was used over and over again in Hardy's work. The Mayor of Casterbridge walked up Cuckoo Lane in search of Farfrae and Wildeve and Thomasin married in Stinsford Church.

Hardy's father was a master-mason but it was his mother, Jemima, who engineered his apprenticeship with John Hicks. In the course of his work on church restoration he visited St Juliot, near Boscastle in Cornwall, where he met his future wife Emma Lavinia Gifford, who urged him to become a full-time writer.

Eventually Hardy designed Max Gate, a house just outside Dorchester, where he produced his greatest work. It has to be remembered, however, that this is the Dorset of Hardy's imagination. Real places and features are enhanced, moved or romanticised to suit the mood of the story.

Emma's death in 1910 provoked a flood of romantic poems. In 1914 he married Florence Emily Dugdale but by now Hardy was an honoured Grand Old Man of literature, visited by royalty and many famous people of the time. He died on the evening of 11th January 1928 at Max Gate.

The selection of pubs used in this book was dependant solely upon their proximity to the paths Hardy walked, the settings for his books, his birthplace, the houses he lived in during his life, the churches he helped restore and his place of worship where his heart and his relatives are buried. There is a photograph and full page report with information regarding accommodation, food, beer and opening times etc. whilst each section includes biographical notes, literary associations and historical interest.

The interesting selection of walks, all circular and accompanied by a sketch map, vary from 2½ - 9½ miles. Although designed to start at or near the pub one can of course begin walking anywhere along the route assured that refreshment will be at hand.

Apart from being immensely enjoyable walking is extremely good for you provided a few simple rules are observed. Wear suitable clothing, lightweight or quick drying trousers are advisable. A waterproof jacket or cagoule is essential so too are strong well-treaded waterproof boots. Take care on lanes where there are no pavements and walk where possible facing the on-coming traffic. If possible take the relevant Ordnance Survey map, a stick for clearing brambles and a torch if walking late into the evening. Always remember the country code; guard against all fires, fasten gates, keep dogs under control, keep to the paths across fields, and do not pick wild flowers.

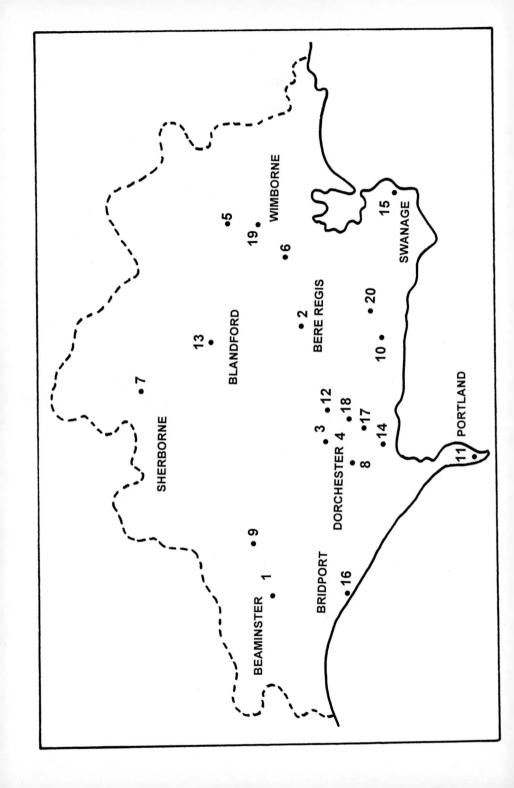

CONTENTS

Walk No. 1

BEAMINSTER
(Emminster)

The Greyhound Inn

Beaminster is much older than many of the present buildings would indicate having suffered two major fires in the 17th century and one in the 18th century. Established in 1760 this popular town centre pub has two main seating areas, one having a flagstone floor, part wood panelled walls and a long dark wood bar. The undulating corridor leads through to a very nice comfortably furnished, low ceilinged family room with a good children's menu above the log effect fire.

The pub is part of the Palmers estate serving three real ales Bridport Bitter, I.P.A. and Tally Ho.

Food is served at lunchtime and in the evening seven days a week. On my last visit the blackboard menu above the fireplace listed the usual snacks of sandwiches, ploughman's, jacket potatoes and home-made soup of the day. Also I noted lentil, hazelnut and mushroom pate, grilled sardines in garlic butter, deep fried crispy coated Camembert with raspberry sauce, goujons of salmon with a garlic and mint dip, half a pint of whole garlic prawns and deep fried longboat potato shells filled with chilli. There were traditional favourites like home-made steak and kidney pie, chicken curry, a large mixed grill, gammon and various steaks plus chicken cordon bleu, grilled whole plaice and lemon sole, seafood crepes filled with smoked haddock and prawns in a white wine sauce and topped with cheese and prawns. Vegetarians are well catered for with dishes like spinach and mushroom lasagne, mushroom and nut fettuccini, cauliflower cheese, country lentil crumble and tomato and vegetable taglitalle. Sweets range from traditional puddings like spotted dick and treacle sponge to fruit pavlova and banana split.

Children in family room, dogs welcome if kept under control.

Opening times 11 - 2 30 and 6 30 - 11. Sunday - 12 - 3 and 7 - 10 30.

Telephone: (01308) 862496.

"Sweet Be'mi'ster, that bist a-bound
By green an' woody hills all round,
Wi' hedges, reachen up between
A thousan' vields o' zummer green..."
William Barnes

Biographical Notes:

Hutchin's 'History & Antiquities of the County of Dorset' (Hardy's copy is much annotated) shows that Tess of the d'Urbervilles, in her walk from Flintcomb-Ash to Beaminster passed through lands once owned by Hardy's ancestors. He was always conscious of the decline of the great county families, and of his own; "So we go down, down, down".

Gertrude Bugler, one of the Hardy players who at Christmas 1920 appeared at Max Gate in costume to perform the mummer's scene of Saint George from 'The Return of the Native', married her cousin, also named Bugler, and settled in Beaminster.

In April 1925 Florence, who was deeply jealous of her husband's admiration for the actress, suddenly appeared at her Beaminster home and begged her to reject any idea of going to London to appear as Tess on stage. She argued that Hardy would insist on going to London and would visit her dressing room and that the ensuing publicity would ruin his nerves and reputation. Florence also told Gertrude that she had destroyed poems from Hardy to her. Gertrude withdrew from the London production but she never forgave Florence for ruining her chances of appearing in the West End.

Literary Associations:

TESS OF THE D'URBERVILLES. When Tess and Angel part, he returns to his parents, the vicar of Beaminster and his wife, to the "hill-surrounded little town" with "the Tudor church-tower of red stone." The Vicarage, on the corner of the lane leading to St Mary's Church, was their home. After working at Flintcomb-Ash for a while, Tess herself decides to call on Angel Clare's parents for news of him. It was a fifteen-mile walk in winter - "the ground ringing under her feet like an anvil..." She leaves her thick boots under a hedge and dons her pretty thin ones of patent leather for the visit. There is no-one at home at the vicarage. While walking back up the hill, Angel's two brothers (who do not know her) overtake her, and with Mercy Chant, the women chosen by their respective parents as a suitable bride for Angel, find Tess's old boots and appropriate them for charity. "Some impostor who wished to come into the town barefoot, per-haps, and so excite our sympathies" says Miss Chant. Tess returns to the farm, defeated.

Walk No. 1

Historical Interest:

On Palm Sunday 1644, during the Civil War when Prince Maurice was quartered there, the town was set on fire and nearly burned to the ground. More fires in 1684 and 1781 did further damage, but the church escaped, with its memorial windows of rich stained glass and its 16th-century tower. A curious building, the Mort House, adjoins the church.

In the past Beaminster was a thriving centre known for rope and sail makers, wrought iron work, paper making, embroidered buttons, shoes, clocks and cheese. A famous resident of the past was Thomas Hine, born in 1775. He went to Cognac, France, in his youth, married the daughter of a brandy merchant and founded 'Connoisseurs' brandy.

Just outside Beaminster lies Parnham House, restored from the 16th-century original, partly by John Nash in the 19th-century. More recently it has become the home of John Makepeace furniture workshops, where craftsmen, including Viscount Linley, Princess Margaret's son, learn to design and make modern furniture using English hardwoods such as holly, mulberry and burr oak.

The grave of William Rhodes Moorhouse, the first airman to be awarded the Victoria Cross, lies on the hillside above. His son, William, a Hurricane pilot in the Second World War, was shot down in 1940, and was awarded the D.F.C. He was buried beside his father.

Parnham House

The Walk:

Beaminster is at the meeting point of the A3066 and B3163 7 miles north of Bridport.

Approximate distance: 4 miles. OS Map 193 ST 481/014.

Pay and display car park opposite.

A very scenic rural walk across farm land to Parnham House returning along tracks and country lanes. Although a little hilly at times the walk is not demanding but can be wet in places during the winter.

1. From the inn turn right, cross the road and turn left walking down towards the church. Take the next left passing the Old Vicarage on the corner and follow the lane past all the dwellings and join the track ahead. Pass through the gate and keep straight-ahead then leave the track and fork right in the direction of the bridleway post. Pass through the gate and maintain your direction ahead

across the field to the stile and further on fork right.

2. If you want to visit Parnham House fork left and return back up the path to the bridleway. Open from April to October on Tuesdays, Wednesday, Thursdays, Sundays and Bank Holidays 10 a.m. to 5 p.m. present charge adults £4 children £2. Walk past the bluebell woods and turn right at the cross track. Carry on up the hill from which you have a lovely view of the surrounding countryside. Pass through the gate and keep straight ahead, at the bend go through the gate and across the field to the stile following the narrow track ahead down to the lane and turn right.

3. Almost immediately turn left into the driveway to Higher Arrowfield Farm. Walk past the dwelling, over the metal stile into the field and turn right around the out buildings then left at the next metal stile. Halfway down the field climb the stile on the right, walk across to the steps and turn left through the industrial estate and out into the road.

4. Cross to the path opposite signposted, Horn Hill 1 mile. Walk round and out into the industrial estate turning left along the track. Pass between the farm buildings and keep

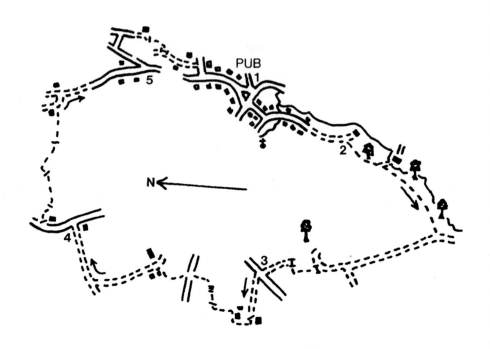

straight ahead, through the brook following the often muddy but attractive bluebell lined track ahead. The track widens and after passing a bluebell wood on the right turn right at the path junction following the grass track up and out into the road turning left.

4. Keeping to the verge on the left walk up and round the bend crossing over just past the entrance to the dwelling and further on climb the stile into the field. Bear right over to a pair of stiles in the hedge and, keeping close to the hedge on the left walk down the field to the stile in the corner. Cross into the field and bear

right over to the crossing point and, keeping close to the hedge on the right, walk round to the gap, out to the track turn right and right again at the thatched cottage.

5. Turn left into the lane at the bottom, walk uphill past the cul-de-sac and take the next right. Cross the stream, turn right and walk up to the dwelling. The footpath is on the right between the hedge and the tennis court. After passing through the gate bear right across the field to the metal kissing gate in the hedge, go out onto the tarred track, turn left then right and left again into Fleet Street back to the pub.

BERE REGIS
(Kingsbere)
WOODBURY HILL
(Greenhill)

The Drax Arms

By-passed a few years ago tranquillity has once more returned to this ancient Dorset village its roots far back in the mist of time. In Saxon times Queen Alfrida came here to atone with a life of contrition for whatever part she played in the murder of young Edward at Corfe Castle in 979. King John once lived here so did the founder of our parliament, Simon de Montfort.

Very much a village local the Drax Arms occupies a sunny position in the centre of the village. A wood burning stove heats one side of the main bar, devoted to pub games whilst the dining area at the opposite end has rustic furniture and a large open fireplace with a grate on a raised heath. There are a few seats on the sheltered rear patio and beyond that picnic benches on a raised lawn.

Well run by the tenants the pub is owned by Hall and Woodhouse stocking three of their real ales, Badger Best, I.P.A. and Tanglefoot.

Weekday food times are from 12 noon - 2 00 and 6.30 - 9. Saturday 12 noon - 2.30 and 6.30 - 9.30 (Sunday 7 - 9). A typical range of snacks listed on the blackboard might included ploughman's, jacket potatoes, plain and toasted sandwiches, beef burgers or starters such as deep fried Brie, Ardennes pate, vegetable spring roll, garlic mushrooms and seafood cocktail. A selection of basket meals include scampi, breaded plaice, venison sausages, home baked ham, egg and chips, gammon and rump steak. I noted on my last visit that melon with Port headed the specials board followed by lasagne, vegetable bake, a large mixed grill, Barnsley lamb chop, local trout stuffed with celery and walnuts and a roast beef salad.

Weekday opening times 11 - 2.30 (4 p.m. Saturday) & 6 - 11. Sunday 12 noon - 4.00 and 7 - 10.30.

Children welcome and dogs on a lead.

Telephone: (01929) 471386.

11

"Under the hill, and just ahead of them, was the
half-dead townlet of their pilgrimage, Kingsbere..."
TESS OF THE D'URBERVILLES.

Biographical Notes:

In 1873 Hardy walked from Bockhampton to Woodbury Hill fair, a distance of 13 miles. In September 1880, he heard a curious piece of family gossip. His mother's grandfather, William Hand, worried about his property so much that he would call on his lawyer in Bere Regis to alter his will almost every fortnight. A relative used to drive him there and back and worked on William so assiduously that he eventually got three-quarters of the property, including the houses bequeathed to himself.

At Christmas in 1890, Hardy recorded another piece of gossip in his notebook. Mr Hibbs of Bere Regis told him that a native of that place, now 90, says he remembers a young woman doing penance in Bere Church for singing scandalous songs about "a great lady". The girl stood in a white sheet while she went through "the service of penance...". The source of the d'Urbervilles of the story was the genealogy of the Turberville family Hardy found in his searches through Hutchin's THE HISTORY AND ANTIQUITIES OF THE COUNTY OF DORSET, and visits to the church at Bere Regis.

Literary Associations:

Most famously, Bere Regis church is where Tess found the relics of her supposed ancestors. "Kingsbere, the spot of all spots in the world which could be considered the d'Urbervilles home, since they had resided there for full five hundred years." They arrive in the town to find their room had been let, so they unloaded the furniture outside the church and erected the old four-poster bed under the south wall, "the part of building known as the d'Urberville Aisle, beneath which the huge vaults lay." In the traceried window above were the heraldic emblems like those they had seen on her father's old seal and spoon.

Kingsbere also figures in FAR FROM THE MADDING CROWD. THE DYNASTS, and THE TRUMPET MAJOR, and a poem "The Alarm", but in these most of the action takes place at Woodbury Hill (Greenhill). Here Bathsheba's soldier husband, Troy, thought to have been drowned, reappears performing Dick Turpin in the circus act. Here Gabriel Oak drives his sheep for sale and poor Joseph Poorgrass, the bashful rural philosopher who suffers on occasions from "the multiplying eye" is taken to the fair to cure his shyness.

The Church at Bere Regis

Walk No. 2

Historical Interest:

Bere Regis - A medieval town associated with Kings John, Henry III and Edward I. The church has been rebuilt several times, finally by Henry VII's Lord Chancellor, Cardinal Morton. On his death in 1500 the manor reverted to the King and then passed to the Turberville family. The parish register contains an original signature of Tho. Turberville dated May ye 10th 1679.

Woodbury Hill - Originally an ancient British or Belgic-British camp. Legend has it that the fair was started by a packman caught in a thunderstorm. Soaked through, he climbed the hill and spread his wares out on the grass to dry. Some of the villagers of Bere Regis saw him and climbed the hill out of curiosity and purchased all his stock. On the same day in subsequent years he repeated this operation and other vendors joined in and it turned into an annual fair. At its height it lasted three weeks. The first day was called "gentlefolks' day" and the last "pack and penny day". After 1914 the fair was no longer important for the sale of livestock, and it ceased to exist after World War II.

During the Napoleonic Wars, the civilian population was instructed to evacuate the coast and make for Bere Regis. The order for this retreat still exists in the Dorset Record Office. They were warned by the lighting of beacons on high points in the county.

A view of the village from Woodbury Hill

The Walk:

Village just south of the junction of the A35 and A31. Pub in West Street.

Approximate distance: 5½ miles. OS Map 194 SY 846/948.

Park anywhere in the village.

This extremely enjoyable walk, one of my personal favourites takes you first to the church then along a lovely riverside path before climbing a steep track to join a lovely path through bluebell woods. After passing through the remote and peaceful hamlet of Turners Puddle a bridleway track rises through woods and crosses open heath before descending through more woods to the village. An optional climb takes you high up onto Woodbury Hill with lovely views across the village. It is a fairly long walk but the going is generally good underfoot mostly on well-established paths and bridleways and although a little strenuous in places is quite suitable for all members of the family.

1. Leave the pub and turn left shortly turning right into Church Lane. Walk round the church, out through the rear gate, down to the road and turn right. Keep going until you reach the short track on the left leading to the scout hut and just before the hut join the signed footpath on the right. This very attractive path and boardwalk passes through an area of wet woodland before reaching a bridge on the left. Cross to the opposite bank and turn right.

2. At the track turn left, walk up to the corner and bear right into the field, cross to the far side and turn

15

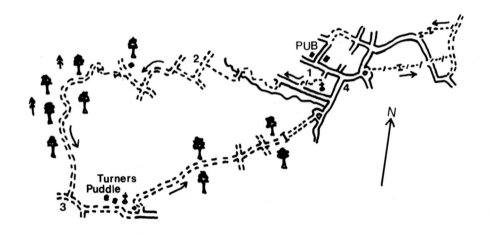

left. The track rises quite steeply allowing good views back across the village. Turn right upon reaching the cross track, walk up to the farm buildings and pass through the small metal gate into the field on the left. Bearing right make for the gate in the far corner and enter the bluebell wood following this very attractive path as it winds its way down through the woods and along a field path to a track.

3. Turn left (fingerpost indicates Throop and Turners Puddle). Keep straight ahead into the small hamlet of Turners Puddle, past the church and just beyond the farm buildings on the left join the signed bridleway. After rounding the farm the track rises steadily through attractive woodland and crosses open heath. Keep straight ahead crossing two gravel paths then follow the path down through woods to an oak enclo-

sure. Go down the steep bank and make for the gate opposite following the track ahead, past the dwellings into the road and turn left. Walk back to the village either turning left to the pub or right to climb Woodbury Hill.

4. Cross the road by the roundabout and join the narrow signed path crossing stiles and fields before turning right into the lane. Walk up and round turning left onto the gravel track. Go past the dwellings and join the signed bridleway on the left. Bearing right walk across to the trees and down to the gate in the corner, through a second, out into the lane and turn right. Cross the road to the gate, keep straight ahead, then left by the letterbox and immediately turn right up the gravel track. After passing through the back of the village finally fork left down Snow Hill to the pub.

CHARMINSTER
(Charmley)

The Inn for
All Seasons

This two-storey, white painted cottage pub originally known as the New Inn was renamed after major refurbishment. Part wood stained panelled walls and a stained wood panelled bar are strong features in the attractive linked front bars. Displayed on and around the two open brick fireplaces are various antique copper and brass items, a bracket clock and old prints of Weymouth. At the back is a very attractive large dining room, a skittle alley/function room, a riverside garden and children's play area

The inn is a freehouse, which last changed hands in the middle of 1997. The new owners offer a good selection of real ales which presently include Popes Traditional and Royal Oak from Eldridge Pope, Fuller's London Pride and Otter Bitter.

Good imaginative food can be ordered every day of the week from 12 noon - 2.30 and 6.30 - 9.30. The printed menu lists traditional ploughman's, French sticks and old time favourites like home cooked ham egg and chips and vegetarian dishes such as asparagus crepes topped with cheese sauce and a home-made fruit and nut pilaf. Starters which include home-made soup, Dorset pate and Mediterranean salad - tomatoes, onion and watercress topped with tuna and a dressing are followed by a large range of fish dishes. On my last visit the specials on offer included pan fired duck breast with fresh mango puree, noisettes of kangaroo fillet with brandy, a skate wing, mixed grill, a large native sea bass steamed and served with salad, also home-made faggots in a rich gravy, fresh whole lemon sole, home-made quiche and tenderloin of pork chops with bramley apple sauce and Stilton. There is a good children's menu.

Four letting rooms one with a four poster.

Opening times 11 - 3 (12 noon Sunday) and 6.30 - 11.

Children and dogs equally welcome.

Telephone: (01305) 264694.

Walk No. 3

*"In going out of Casterbridge by the low-lying road which eventually
conducts to the town of Ivell, you see on the right hand an ivied
manor-house, flanked by battlemented towers, and more than usually
distinguished by the size of its many mullioned windows"*

Dame the Eighth. The Lady Penelope.
From A GROUP OF NOBLE DAMES

Charmley is mentioned in UNDER THE GREENWOOD TREE. It is the village
Dick Dewy visited to assist at the funeral of one of his friends, (In the glossary
of place names Charmley is not mentioned and it is possible that the name is
imaginary and not an equivalent for Charminster.)

Biographical Notes:

The powerful Trenchard family had a l anch in Dorset. The back of their town
house, known as Trenchard Mansio.., had extended into Shire Hall Lane
Dorchester, (where Hardy rented a house while Max Gate was being built).
This was pulled down circa 1848. Thomas mentioned the house in his speech
accepting the freedom of Dorchester in 1910. This branch of the Trenchards
had their estate at Wolfeton House on the outskirts of Charminster.

Literary Associations:

Wolfeton House figures largely in A GROUP OF NOBLE DAMES. Dame the
Eighth, The Lady Penelope, lived there. In the parish church of Charminster
there is a tomb marking the spot where the Lady Penelope and her last

Wolfeton House

husband are buried. In the fictional story the Lady is wooed by three suitors. "Only bide your time quietly" she tells them "and, in faith, I will marry you all in turn." And, in faith, she does. Sir George Drenghard the most elderly and her first choice of husband, a few months after their wedding "died of his convivialities". Sir William, her next best beloved had gone abroad so she settled for Sir John Gale and a very unhappy second marriage. He too became ill and died but Lady Penelope was loathe to rush into marriage with Sir William Hervy, with good reason. Rumour and gossip spread after these very convenient deaths and Lady Penelope herself succumbed - "done to death by a vile scandal".

Historical Interest:

Hardy always maintained that these stories were based on fact. Penelope Darcy, second daughter of Lord Darcy of Chirk, Viscount Colchester and Earl Rivers was a very rich young lady. She was also to inherit estates of her mother, the daughter of Sir Thomas Kitson. The following is the true story of the Lady Penelope. She did indeed have three suitors who planned to bid for her hand by means of jousting and archery. Penelope forbade this and told she would become the wife of each in turn. This was in about 1625. First she married 50-years old Sir George Trenchard of Wolfeton. (Hardy did not show much imagination in changing the names.) He died within a year and she married Sir John Gage. A few years later he also died and she married the youngest suitor, Sir William Harvey.

There is a Spanish connection. In January 1506, on their way back to Spain to claim the throne for Joan of Arragon, Archduke Philip of Austria and his wife 'mad Joan of Spain' were swept ashore at Weymouth during a storm. Sir Thomas Trenchard rescued them and escorted them to the safety of Wolfeton House. Sir Thomas spoke no Spanish so he sent for young John Russell from Berwick, near Bridport. When the Archduke and his wife were invited to Windsor, Russell went with them and subsequently founded the dynasty of the Dukes of Bedford. Philip and Joan rewarded the Trenchards' kindness with a gift of two Chinese porcelain bowls, said to be the first to have reached England.

There is another gruesome legend connected with the house. A Justice had been invited to dine there. No sooner had they all sat down to eat when he suddenly ordered his carriage and left the house. He told the Marshal with him that he had seen standing behind Lady Trenchard's chair, a ghostly figure of herself with her throat cut and her head under her arm. Before the Justice and his escort had reached Dorchester, a mounted messenger caught up with their carriage and told him that Lady Trenchard had committed suicide.

Walk No. 3

The Walk:

Charminster is signed just north of Dorchester from the A352.

Approximate distance: 3½ miles. OS Map 194 SY 678/927.

Park at the pub or in the lane opposite.

A fairly short but interesting walk at first beside the Cerne river and through the small historic village of Charminster towards Wolfeton House then along attractive field paths, farm tracks and a green lane. Generally good underfoot the walk is ideal for all members of the family.

1. Leave the pub turning left and shortly turn left into the drive. Cross the stile into the field making for the kissing gate in the bottom right-hand corner then turn right along the riverside path, through the churchyard to the road and turn left. Walk up East Hill turning right at the top then fork right at the bend. After passing the dwellings go as far as the signed footpath on the left. The drive ahead leads to Wolfeton House. It is privately owned but will open to the public from May 1st on Mondays, Tuesdays and Thursdays between 2 p.m. - 6 p.m. There will be a small admission charge.

2. Keep to this narrow path then follow the track beside the hedge down to the stile and straight ahead across the field to the farm yard, out into the lane and turn left. Cross the road and almost immediately pass through the gate into the field bearing left to the

stile beside the building. Go down the steps and keep straight ahead beside the fence to the stile and up the track ahead signposted, Higher Burton ½. Ignore the signed footpath on the left but keep walking towards the farm turning left between the buildings and over the stile into the field. Bearing right cross to the stile in the hedge, then over to the gate, down then up to the stile, across the playing fields and out through the kissing gate into the road.

3. Turn left and then right into Vicarage Lane. Walk for a while and then take the footpath on the right signposted, to Herrison. Keep straight ahead along this delightful shaded path eventually crossing the stile into the field and make for the gate in the far top corner. Keep to the path bearing left and upon reaching the fingerpost turn left walking down the hillside making you way towards and behind the thatched cottage. Pass through the gate and turn left along the track. Walk to the end and turn right and finally when you reach the kissing gate re-trace your steps up the field back to the pub.

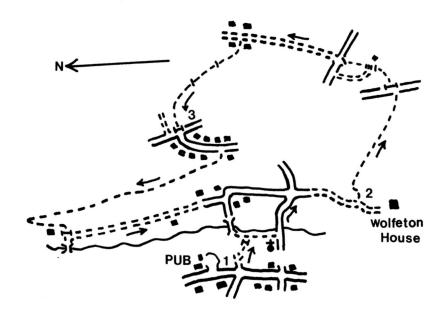

Walk No. 4

DORCHESTER
(Casterbridge)

The Kings Arms
Dorchester

It is said that an inn has occupied this site since the Middle Ages but the first mention was 1618 when the landlord was one William Aberconary. The inn was a major coaching stop when the journey to London took all of 15 hours. Thomas Hardy regularly ate here.

The lounge bar is divided into three main areas with a low heavily beamed section by the bar. Pictures compete for space on the walls whilst other interesting artefacts including stuffed fish occupy the remaining shelf space. Beyond the comfortable restaurant there is a lovely conservatory.

This well managed Inn is a Premier Lodge, part of the Greenalls Group. Real ale drinkers have a choice of four Draught Bass, Tetleys, Directors Bitter and Flowers Original.

Very good bar food available all week between 12 noon and 2.30 and from 6 - 9. Sunday 12 noon - 2.30 and 7 - 9.30, ranges from snacks such as sandwiches, baguettes and ploughman's to old favourites such as steak and kidney pie and pan fried lambs liver and bacon whilst the specials board could include a Kings club sandwich - a triple decker toasted with ham, tomato, mustard, turkey, lettuce and mayonnaise. Also listed are braised steak and onions, salmon and broccoli bake, beef paprika - tender strips of beef cooked in paprika and tomato sauce and chicken Italienne - pan fried chicken cooked with tomatoes, peppers, onions, mushroom and herbs. There are children's meals and a Sunday roast. Henry's Table lists a large comprehensive selection samples of which include Cointreau and orange pate and tempura chicken also vegetarian aubergine, mozzarella and parmesan bake.

Weekday opening times Monday - Thursday 11 - 3 and 6 - 11, Friday all day 11 - 11 and Sunday 12 noon - 3 and 7 - 10.30.

No objection to children and dogs

Hotel accommodation in 33 en-suite bedrooms

Telephone: (01305) 265353 Fax: (01305) 260269.

"... a mosaic-work of subdued reds, browns, greys,
and crystals, held together by a rectangular frame
of deep green."
THE MAYOR OF CASTERBRIDGE

Biographical Notes:
Hardy sent to the Dorchester British School, Headmaster Isaac Last in 1849.
1856-61, articled to John Hicks, architect, 39 South Street.
1856 - witnessed the hanging of Martha Brown in public at the gates of Dorchester prison.
10 August 1858 - watched Seale being hanged outside Dorchester gaol - the last man to be hanged in public in England.
June 1883 - moved to Dorchester, rents house in Shire Hall Lane. Bought plot of land from the Duchy of Cornwall to build a house.
June 29 1885 - moved into Max Gate on the Wareham road.
July 1901 - Hardy elected member of the Restoration Committee to advise on the partial rebuilding of Fordington St George's Church.
16 November 1910 - Hardy was awarded the Freedom of the Borough of Dorchester.
21 July 1927 - his last public appearance to lay commemoration stone of the new Dorchester Grammar School.
11 January 1928 - Died at Max Gate.

Literary Associations:
Dorchester is best known as the setting for THE MAYOR OF CASTERBRIDGE, published in 1886. For some sites he used their real names -

St Peter's Church, with William Barnes' statue outside, contains the Hardy Chapel at the end of the south aisle, ancient Hardys he claimed as his ancestors.

The King's Arms - where Henchard's wife Susan and her daughter, Elizabeth-Jane, the wife he sold at a country fair some years previously, found him presiding over a dinner surrounded by Councillors.

Susan Henchard took temporary lodgings over the china shop next door to Judge Jeffrey's lodgings.

Walk No. 4

The Antelope Hotel - a 17th century hostelry still stands on South Street, opposite to the place where Henchard's house was supposed to be situated.

The Napper's Mite - also in South Street, was an almshouse in Hardy's time.

North Square - (previously Bullstake Square) has lost the stone post in the centre where once the bulls were tethered.

High Place Hall - Lucetta's home, drawn from Colliton House. The arch and mask mentioned in the story did exist but are now in the County Museum decorating the door to the library.

Mill Lane - (Mixen Lane in the story) was considerably cleaned up even in Hardy's time and now bears no resemblance to the squalid district it once was.

Maumbury Rings - (The Ring) a Roman amphitheatre is still there outside the town.

William Barnes   The Napper's Mite

Maumbury Rings

Poundbury - (Pummery) is better known today as the site of Prince Charles' model village.

The Swan Bridge, Grey's Bridge and the Cornmarket - feature in several of Hardy's works as well as THE MAYOR OF CASTERBRIDGE, notably FAR FROM THE MADDING CROWD.

His short story 'The Withered Arm' features the old gaol and the Hangman's Cottage, a thatched building now a private house, beside the Frome.

Many of Hardy's poems, 'The Burghers', 'Her Death and After', 'Bereft', etc. include Dorchester scenes, especially Fordington (Durnover).

Historical Interest:
Many Roman remains. Roman town house displayed in Colliton Park (behind the Council offices)

Hardy found Roman remains at Max Gate when the foundations were dug.

Two Roman aqueducts only are known in the British Isles, one of which starts to the west of Poundbury.

Walk No. 4

At St George's, Fordington, a Roman tombstone can be seen in the inner tower wall of the church.

Judge Jeffreys' "Bloody Assizes" took place in the oak room at the back of the Antelope Hotel. 74 men were executed as a result of the Monmouth Rising.

The Roman amphitheatre at Maumbury originated as a sacred Neolithic enclosure dating back probably before 2000 BC. The public gallows stood here until 1767.

The Walk:

Pub on the right in the main road through the town.

Approximate distance: 2½ miles. OS Map 194 SY 695/907.

There is a car park at the rear of the pub plus ample public car parks close by. 1-hour parking restrictions are lifted in the High Street on Sunday.

A leisurely town centre stroll, ideal for a fine Sunday afternoon which includes an attractive riverside walk and explores the quieter areas and open spaces within this ancient market town.

1. From the front entrance turn right, walk up through the centre of the town turning right into Clyde Path Road. The site of Hardy's house is on the left. Carry on down the hill until you reach the bend then go down the steps on the right, cross the bridge over the stream and turn right following the path along the bank. After passing the allotments a board walk on the left loops through a wet nature reserve returning to the path a few steps further on. Continue along the path eventually reaching the main road.

2. Cross over and join the path opposite beside the stream and when you reach the bridge on the right cross to the far side, bear left up the slope to the road, turn right and then left up Pound Lane. Turn left into the road at the top towards Fordington Church. Take the next right into Fordington Green, and keeping to the right-hand side of the road carry on down past the houses and up the raised path turning right into Salisbury Fields.

3. At the end of Salisbury Street turn left into Durngate Street walking until you reach Cornhill then turn left into South Street. The building on the left, presently occupied by Barclays' Bank, is the house reputed to be lived in by The Mayor of Casterbridge. Further down on the left is The Nappers Mite - an almhouse in Hardy's time.

4. At the end of the road bear right into Weymouth Avenue, up past the brewery to the top of the road and into Maumbury Rings on the left. This rare Neolithic monument known as a 'henge' dates back to 2500 BC. After 800 years of neglect the Romans converted it to an amphi-

26

theatre in the 1st century AD but it is was out of use by AD 150. From June 1642 to June 1643 it was an artillery fort guarding the southern approach to Dorchester by Parliamentary supporters. Continue up the road turning right just before the traffic lights into Maumbury Road. Cross over into Cornwall Road and immediately join the footpath on the right signposted,

Tourist Information and Town Centre. Bear left into West Walks following the path along the edge of the park past some lovely period houses and out into the road at the top. On the right is a small section of the original Roman wall. Hardy's statue can be seen on the corner opposite the main road. Turn right down High West Street back to the Inn.

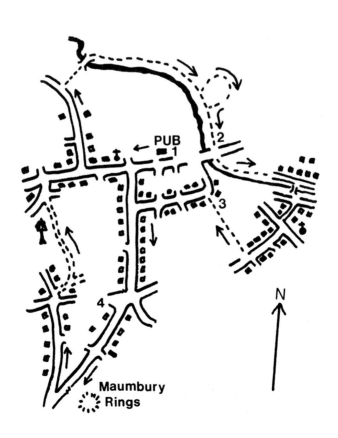

Walk No. 4

Dorchester

Fordington Church

HORTON & HINTON
MARTELL

The Horton Inn
(Lornton Inn)

Historically Horton is recorded as the place where the unfortunate Duke of Monmouth was captured together with his two companions Lord Grey and a German officer named Buyse having fled to the area after his defeat at Sedgemoor in Somerset.

Occupying an open position at Horton Cross the Horton Inn, originally an old 18th century coaching stop was the place Thomas Hardy had in mind as the rendezvous for his eloping heroine in the Old Surgeon's macabre story in The Nobel Dames collection. Today it is a comfortable inn with an excellent candlelit restaurant, a well appointed bar heated by an open log fire. Tables, chairs and picnic benches are neatly positioned outside on the sunny front terrace.

A good selection of wines, two ciders and real ales are always available in this freehouse which presently include Ringwood Best and True Glory, Flowers Original and King Alfred Bitter also guest beers from time to time.

The extensive bar menu supplemented with daily specials such as venison, pheasant, shark steak, stir fried chicken and coq-au-vin is available every day from 12 noon - 9.30. Presently listed are garlic mushrooms, deep fried Camembert, moules mariniere, smoked duck breast and a warm beef salad followed by peppercorn pork, supreme of chicken, rack of lamb, supreme of salmon, fish medley, hunters porterhouse steak and noisettes of lamb. Vegetarians can choose between mushroom stroganoff and sweet pepper and mangetout stir fry served with honey and soy dressing. Afternoon clotted cream teas

The inn is open all day every day from 11 - 11 (Sunday 12 noon - 10.30) Families and dogs welcome.

Ten bedrooms, 7 en suite all having tea making facilities and colour TV. Telephone: (01258) 840252. Fax: (01258) 841400.

Walk No. 5

*"He reached the solitary wayside tavern
called Lorton Inn - the rendevous of many
a daring poacher for operations
in the adjoining forest..."*
Barbara of the House of Grebe

Biographical Notes:

Hardy had been sent home to Dorset after a spell in London, due to failing health. When the architect Hardy trained with died in February 1869, his out-standing work, mainly church restoration, was undertaken by Crickmay of Weymouth and Hardy was persuaded to stay in Dorset and help him out. The plaque in the church porch states that Hardy helped in the design and super-vision of the re-building of Hinton Martell Church in 1870 but most of his work was completed before this time. He was living in Weymouth, returning to Bockhampton for the weekends, and busily writing DESPARATE REMEDIES, his first published novel. 1870 was also the year when in March he was sent to Cornwall to survey a church at St Juliot and met his first wife, Emma Lavinia Gifford.

Hardy may well have come to know Horton Inn during this time but the houses used as settings in BARBARA OF THE HOUSE OF GREBE he visited later in his life when he lived at Wimborne 1881-1883.

Literary Associations:

The inn plays an important part of BARBARA OF THE HOUSE OF GREBE, one of the short stories collected as A GROUP OF NOBLE DAMES. At the time in which the story is set, Horton Inn (Lornton) stood on the main turnpike road connecting Poole (Havenpool), Wimborne (Warborne) and Salisbury (Melchester), a branch of the road known then as the Great Western Highway.

The mansion of the Earl (Lord Uplanders) is based on Wimborne St Giles, seat of the earls of Shaftesbury. The home of Barbara, Chene Manor, Canford Manor, is now Canford School. Hardy visited Lord Wimborne at Canford in December 1881 and the descriptions of the interior, especially John o'Gaunts kitchen, are from sight. There is no evidence that Hardy visited St Giles, but the 9th Earl of Shaftesbury joined the Prince of Wales with a party of people who lunched at Max Gate in July 1923.

Barbara falls in love with a penniless artisan, a glass painter from Shottsford (Blandford), a detail of local history. Glass painting is correctly described as an important industry in the town. He is sent abroad to receive an education appropriate to her station in life and returns badly burned, injured in a fire in Venice. Lornton Inn is the scene of their original plans for elopement and where she waited in vain for his return. He turned up later and she found she could not bear the sight of his injuries. Much later, after he returned abroad and was presumed dead, she met Lord Uplandtowers, again at Lornton Inn, and eventually married him.

Historical Interest:
Hinton Martell: During the rebuilding of the church, a 15th century pilgrim's costrel, or water bottle was found. It can be seen behind a grille in the wall of the tower. Although Hardy was later to express remorse about Victorian restoration, it is a fact that without renovation the church would not have survived. As much of the old material as possible was preserved here, the exterior old iron sundial gnomon and the stone inscription: "Wm. Redman 1636 RIP" statues of St John and Our Lady and carved corbels of a king and queen under the arch of the east window. Inside the oldest possession is a 13th century Purbeck stone font.

Barbara is clearly based on Barbara Webb, daughter of Sir John Webb of Canford Manor. A report in the "Salisbury & Winchester Journal, East Dorset Supplement" for July 31st 1786, details an entertainment Sir John Webb gave for "his tenants and neighbours at his family seat at Canford in Dorset on the marriage of his daughter Miss B Webb with the Earl of Shaftesbury." Two fat bullocks were roasted, there were other viands and "an ocean of punch and strong beer", the common people were entertained in the adjoining meadows while select parties were received in the mansion house, etc..."And on Saturday another most elegant entertainment of a similar nature was given by his lordship's friends at St Giles. Two large oxen and several sheep were roasted whole and upwards of 30 hogs's heads of strong beer and a profusion of wines and other liquors were given."
`

Whether Hardy's story of a very unhappy marriage, the birth of numerous children, all of which died young, is true, one cannot say.

Horton Inn was in those days a very ordinary country wayside tavern with "not much accommodation for a lady". It was redesigned and decorated under the supervision of David Hicks and now caters for a different clientele.

Walk No. 5

The Walk:

The inn is situated on the B3078 at the Horton crossroads about 5 miles north from Wimborne.

Approximate distance: 5 miles. OS Map 195 SU 017/086.

There is a large parking area at the pub also a small area of verge opposite.

One of the most scenic walks in the area which takes you through the beautiful Crichel Park Estate where you have a good view of the House and lake and through the tranquil villages of Hinton Martell and Chalbury. Not over demanding the walk for the most part is on well-surfaced tracks and farm land with short sections along the highway. Although mostly good underfoot certain areas can become very muddy in winter.

1. Leave the inn turning right, and keeping to the right-hand side of the road carefully walk down the hill, over the bridge and take the gravel track on the left beside the Stanbridge Pumping Station. Further on keep straight ahead through the gate steadily walking up this often-muddy track. After passing the farm turn left at the cross track passing the mill. Further on cross the bridge and turn right, walk past the dwelling and keep straight ahead at the next junction turning right after passing the barn to join the attractive woodland path beyond the gate.

2. Cross the bridge, fork left over a second keeping to the track ahead. During the hurricane many mature trees were lost but I am glad to see considerable new planting has taken place. Pass through the white painted kissing gate and along the track from which you have a good view of Crichel House across the lake. Turn left at the drive, past the playing fields, out through the gatehouse and turn left towards New Town.

3. Walk the length of the village and join the narrow path at the back of the old Witchampton Board Mill (shortly to be demolished and replaced with housing). Cross the stile into the field, walk to the one opposite and turn right following the grass tracked bridleway up to the road and turn right.

4. Keeping to the grass verge on the right walk until you reach the dwelling at which point cross into the lane opposite. Turn left at the road junction into the village of Hinton Martell. Fork left at the pond, up past the church climbing the hill until you reach the signposted footpath on the left. Go up the bank to the stile, turn right and follow the fenced path steeply up the hillside, across a couple of stiles and into the field bearing right up to the stile near the top of the hedge on the left. The fenced path (often very muddy) skirts the field, dips to a plank bridge then rises to a stile. Cross the field to the stile, pass through the kissing gate into the churchyard, walk round to the front gate and turn left (good views).

5. Keep straight ahead along the road then almost immediately fork right signposted, Horton Inn 1¼. Walk

Crichel House

Hinton Martell Church

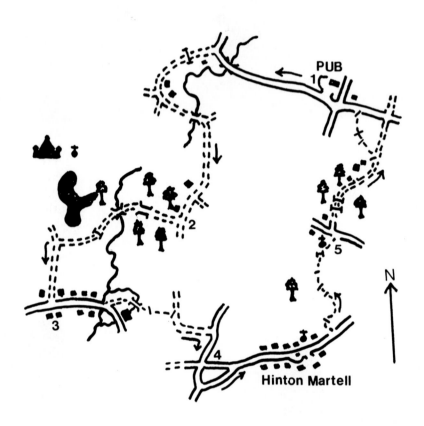

down through the wooden gate then through a second gate into the wood. Keep to the main track, and after passing Chalbury Farm Cottages cross the stile into the field on the left. Either bear right across the field or walk round to the stile, climb into the adjoining field then over the pair of stiles into the field on the left. Bearing right go down to the stile in the far hedge turning left back to the pub.

LYTCHETT
MATRAVERS
& Charborough
Tower
(Welland House)

The Chequers

In 1505 the Black Death almost wiped out the village but found a saviour in Margaret Clements who helped build it all up again. There is a little brass inscription to her in the church near the font, which is decorated with badges of the famous who worshipped here. Among them is a rudder and a fret, not unlike a gridiron, the sign of the Maltravers who gave the village its name.

The exterior belies the age of the popular village pub it is not until you enter the side door that it becomes obvious. Solid leaning walls support the very low beamed ceiling, whilst the cosy alcoves at the front provide an ideal atmosphere for intimate conversation. The Chequers has always been popular I remember visiting the pub in my late teens to listen to country music and drink locally made country wine. Improvements over the years have seen the addition of a large sunny conservatory for family dining and additional bar area at the rear.

The inn is part of Greenalls presently offering a choice of two real ales Draught Bass and Tetley Bitter.

Typical food on the printed menu includes assorted ploughman's, tasty pies, various sandwiches, breaded plaice, scampi, basket meals, curry, jacket potatoes, garlic mushrooms and prawn brochettes - a mixture of tiger prawns, asparagus, and baby sweetcorn in a light tempura sauce. Fair play feast is a surprise selection for two with 2 dips and salad garnish. There is a separate children's menu.

Weekday opening time Monday to Friday 11 - 2 30 and 6 - 11 Sat 11 - 3 Sunday 12 - 3 and 7 - 10.30

Dogs in bar only. Children in family room.

Telephone: (01202) 622215.

*"....the pillar rose into the sky a bright
and cheerful thing ...."*
TWO ON A TOWER

Biographical Notes:
Whilst living in Wimborne, Hardy heard the story of the Drax heiress who married a man twelve years her junior, from a garrulous wagon driver, who drove the party past Charborough Park where he saw the tower. On arriving in Wimborne he and Emma, on their first night at Lanherne, saw Tebbutt's comet overhead. So the theme for TWO ON A TOWER was born.

Literary Associations:
Charborough Park is, roughly, Welland Park, although Hardy has taken some liberties with the description and position of the tower, and the railway connections. Hardy himself tells us that the tower is based on Charborough tower but placed in the setting of the obelisk at Weatherby Castle, near Milborne St Andrew. The tower at Charborough is round but Gothic in style, not Tuscan as Hardy describes and the open observation platform at the top is purely imaginary. Imaginary, too, is the turnpike road between the house and tower. The house is the prototype of the house of the story, but internal descriptions are purely fictional. Hardy did not visit the house until 1927 when he and his second wife, Florence, were invited to lunch. Two miles of brick wall separate the estate from the road, with three entrances, Lion Gate, Almer and Stag Gate. The statue of a stag over the second was sculpted with five legs so that it looks anatomically correct from all angles. The house at one time was close to a village, which became depopulated. Little Welland village in the book appears to be modelled on Winterborne Zelstone. The polygonal thatched Lodge Cottage was added in about 1860.

Historical Interest:
The tower was built in 1790. It was struck by lightning in 1838 but rebuilt the following year. The great deer park was extended in the 1840's by John Sawbridge Erle-Drax, the handsome young man who married the older Miss Drax. As far back as records go Charborough has never changed hands by sale but has passed repeatedly though heiresses. John Sawbridge was urged to change his name to Drax and adopt the family arms upon his marriage. The house was built for Sir Walter Erle, the Parliamentarian before 1661. When the King's troops controlled Dorset the house was burned. Stone and timber from Corfe Castle (where Sir Walter defeated Lady Bankes) were used in the reconstruction. After the Restoration a furious Sir Ralph Bankes demanded restitution. This could not really be done and a great beam from the keep of the Castle remains in position supporting a part of the ground floor.

View of the Tower, seen from the walk

The interesting medieval church of St Mary shows where the old village of Lychett Matravers lay before The Black Death. Inside the church, Sir John Maltravers, who murdered King Edward II in 1327, lies buried beneath the north aisle.

Walk No. 6

The Walk:

Village is signed between the A350 and the A31 west of Wimborne.

Approximate distance: 3½ miles OS Map 195 SY 941/957.

The pub has an ample car park but there is space close by in the surrounding roads

Peaceful country lanes and farm tracks bring you to a point where you can view the tower in Charborough Park. An attractive but often muddy woodland path brings you into a lane where a field path leads to the church. Make this a walk for early spring when you will be rewarded by a magnificent display of wild daffodils. Although it can be muddy the going is generally easy ideal for that family day out.

1. From the pub turn right into the road then take the next left into Lime Kiln Road and left again into Castle Farm Road. Fork left at the junction signposted, Luke Farm only. Gently descending the lane is a picture in spring with many violets, primroses, bluebells, daffodils, hartstongue ferns and other native wild flowers. Walk up to the dwellings and turn left towards Lower Luke Farm join the track then go left into the lane and walk up to the road. From here you have the best view of the tower.

2. Cross the road, climb the bank to the stile and head up the field keeping close to the hedge. Upon reaching the stile go into the adjoining field

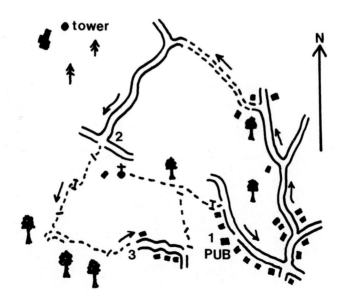

maintaining direction to another stile and straight ahead for twenty paces turning left along the gravel track and enter the bluebell wood (can be muddy). Go over the stile at the end of the path and turn left. If you find the conditions too wet or muddy there is a raised path on the left.

3. Track soon turns to lane and just past the dwellings go over the stile next to the gate on the left. Keep straight ahead over more stiles until you reach the attractive path to the church. The bank on the right and the woods by the church are one of the best places to view wild daffodils. Turn right, walk to the gate at the top then right into the road back to the pub.

Walk No. 7

MARNHULL
(Marlott)

Blackmore Vale Inn

The exterior belies the age of this lovely old pub, which began life 400 years ago. Built originally as farm cottages it later became an old bake house and brew house. Inside there are two very atmospheric bars having heavily beamed ceilings, bare stone walls and two beautiful open inglenook fireplaces housing warm winter fires. There is also a skittle alley, a large beer garden and children's play area.

This well run Hall & Woodhouse tenancy offers a choice of two well conditioned real ales Dorset Best and Tanglefoot.

Very good food can be ordered daily from 11.30 - 1.45 and 6.30 - 10, Sunday 12 noon - 2 and 7 - 8 45. Apart from daily specials like sizzling stir fry meals, fresh fish at weekends and six roasts on Sunday the menu lists a good choice of starters and snacks including home-made soup, mussels cooked in their shells with onion, garlic and parsley and breaded Brie - deep fried and served with fruits of the forest sauce. Main meals include whole grilled plaice and trout, voodoo chicken - breast of chicken filled with cream cheese and chilli stuffing served with spicy tomato and red pepper sauce and chicken en croute. Also listed are game pie and steak and kidney pie, chilli, various grills and a lamb and mango curry. Vegetarians can choose between avocado and corn bake, tortellini ricotta, harvest vegetable and leek pie and pastitsio - Greek style noodle dish of tomatoes, mushrooms, spinach, red peppers, herbs and green peppercorns topped with a cheese sauce.

Children welcome over 8 and dogs on leads.

Weekday opening times 11.30 - 2.30 & 6.30 -11. Sunday 12 noon - 3 & 7 - 10.30

Telephone: (01258) 820701.

'Here, in the valley, the world seems to be constructed upon a smaller and more delicate scale; the fields are mere paddocks, so reduced from this height their hedgerows appear a network of dark green threads overspreading the paler green of the grass.'

TESS OF THE D'URBERVILLES

Biographical Notes:
A favourite walk of Thomas Hardy was from Sturminster Newton to Marnhull. On May 30th 1877 he records making this walk and being entranced by the birdsong. "The prime of bird-singing. The thrushes and blackbirds are the most prominent, - pleading earnestly rather than singing...A bullfinch sings from a tree with a metallic sweetness piercing as a fife."

Literary Associations:
Best known as the birthplace of Tess of the d'Urbervilles, in the Vale of the Little Dairies, "in which the fields are never brown and the springs never dry". "There's a very pretty brew in tap at the Pure Drop, though to be sure, not so good as at Rolliver's", Tess's father told Pa'son Tringham. This parson told John that he was "the lineal representative of the ancient and knightly family of the d'Urbervilles". And it was at Rolliver's the disreputable and illegal drinking house that John learned that there was a rich d'Urberville relation living in Trantridge, and so the tragedy was set in motion.

The Crown, Marnhull

Walk No. 7

The Pure Drop Inn is recognisable as the present Crown Inn near the church. There are two contenders as the origin of Rolliver's. One is Old Lamb House, on the west side of Walton Elm crossroads. Another is The Blackmore Vale, although this has been almost rebuilt since Hardy's day. The Old Rectory, opposite the church, standing behind high forbidding walls, is where Tess pleads with the parson to give her dead baby a Christian burial. He refuses and Tess has eventually to conduct the ceremony herself, burying her child "in that shabby corner of God's allotment where He lets the nettles grow", in St Gregory's churchyard. Marnhull School, built in 1874, is where Tess passes the Sixth Grade, under a London-trained schoolmistress. Hence she learned to speak in two tongues, "the dialect at home, more or less, ordinary English abroad and to persons of quality".

The back lane to Sturminster, on paths following the river, is the way Tess returned home from the Vale of the Great Dairies after leaving Angel Clare. She left her luggage with the turnpike keeper and walked via Cutt Mill and Yardgrove Farm.

Tess's childhood home, which was lost upon her father's death when the lease expired, leaving the family homeless, is now known as Tess Cottage. The building is on the right of the Marnhull to Sturminster road, just north of Walton Elm crossroads. In Hardy's time it was called Barton Cottage. As an elderly man he is reputed to have been seen standing outside and to have told the gardener that he was "only seeing where I put my Tess".

Historical Interest:

In Hardy's era Marnhull supported two breweries and a malthouse and appears to have merited its reputation as "the booziest place in Dorset". It was the largest village in the county and Hardy described it as "long and broken". It is now very much smaller that in its heyday.

Senior's Farm is the oldest house in the village, dating from the early 16th century. It can be found west of the churchyard. The church of St Gregory has a 15th century tower with later 18th century parapet and pinnacles. The Royal Stuart coat of arms appears over the west door.

The name Marnhull is thought to be a corruption of Marl Hill, an earlier name, taken from the white clay or marl occurring in the district. This hardens to a creamy limestone when exposed to the air, and has been used in many local buildings including the church.

About one mile north of the church lies Nash Court, once the residence of Catherine Parr, Henry VIII's widow. In 1795 it became a refuge for 17 Benedictine nuns who escaped from the French Revolution. They were originally taken prisoner but once released, destitute, they came to England and were offered Nash Court by Lady Arundel, then the owner. The inhabitants of Marnhull, however, were deeply suspicious and hostile. The nuns were suspected of being French revolutionaries in disguise, hiding weapons and ammunition and even hiding Napoleon himself. Several times Nash Court was searched and eventually the natives considered themselves justified when a body was discovered buried in the garden. This turned out to be one of the nuns who had died of natural causes but, unfortunately, was buried without the official blessing of a Coroner's inquest. The nuns, tired of the continuing harassment, moved to Bridgwater in Somerset and Marnhull was left in peace.

The Walk:

From the B3092 go past the church into Church Hill and follow the road round through the village.

Approximate distance: 4¾ miles. OS Map 183 ST 774/195.

Park in the road or car park at rear.

An enjoyable mostly level walk guiding you on well trodden field paths to historic Cutt Mill and the village of Hinton St Mary then returning to the village by way of field paths, tracks and farm roads.

1 Turn left from the inn through the village and immediately prior to reaching the road on the right turn right into the drive. Go past the garages, over the stile and bear left around the building to join the gravel track. Walk up to the gate and keep straight ahead following the short grass track up to the stiles. Turn left, over a second stile bearing right in the direction of the waymark. Cross another stile and head up the field on the well trodden path beside the hedge, round the top of the field and through the kissing gate then bear left across to one last kissing gate into the cul-de-sac and down to the road

2. Cross to the lane opposite and continue down the private drive, past the dwelling then go through the little gate on the right, walk around the pond, through two more gates and up into the field. Almost immediately go over the stile on the left then bear right up the field towards the corner of the hedge making for the stile at the top.

3. Turn left into the lane and cross to the farm entrance opposite turning left again along the grass track leading round to a stile. Go round the

43

Walk No. 7

Cutt Mill

The Old Rectory

Pond passed early in the walk

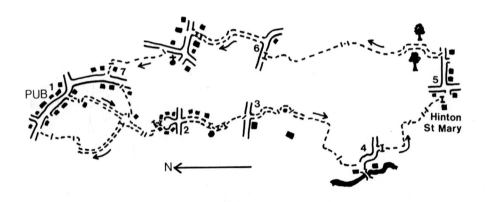

pond keeping straight ahead into the field and across to the pair of stiles in the far hedge. Turn right, enter the next field and continue down and round until you reach the stile then cross to the riverbank and turn left walking towards Cutt Mill. There are good views of the mill from the bridge on the right.

4. Walk up the tarred drive ignoring the signed footpath on the right but continue until you reach the bridle-way signposted, Wood Lane. Go up into the field and turn right past the bluebell wood, through the plantation and the gap in the far hedge. Turn left keeping to the grass strip beside the hedge and when you reach the stile in the wire fence cross into the field on the right. Bear left to the stiles in the hedge then make for the gate between the cottage and out buildings and turn left.

5. Carefully cross the road into the lane opposite walking as far as the stile on the left. Keep to the track

down and round the field, between the plantation and into the field. Walk straight ahead across the length of two fields bearing left at the fence, cross two stiles and a plank bridge and continue round the field to the gate turning right into the lane.

6. Take the next turning left following the concrete farm road up and round the fields, through the farm-yard, out to the road and turn left. Walk past the Crown turning right in front of the church into Church Hill. At the end of the wall cross the stile into the field on the left following the well trodden path across to the gap in the hedge then bear left over to the stile go, up to the road and turn left.

7. Shortly cross the stile into the field on the right and, keeping close to the hedge walk to the gate in the top of the field. Pass through a similar gate on the left, bearing right cross the field to the gate, up the narrow path to the road and turn right back to the pub.

MARTINSTOWN
MAIDEN CASTLE
(Mai-Dun
or Maidon)

The Brewers Arms

Resplendent in summer with an attractive creeper this two-story white painted pub is sited in the main village road beside a stream. Red and green decor pervades throughout the knocked through bar which has part wood panelled walls, comfortable furnishings with a large padded window seat at the front facing a small open fireplace. There is a skittle alley and a vine covered patio together with separate outside catering area also a large seating area at the back with children's play area and some seats at the front looking over the stream a nice spot to sit on a summers evening.

Two real ales presently available are Thomas Greenalls Original and Draught Bass.

Bar meals listed on the menu and available everyday from 12 noon - 10 offer a choice of snacks such as jacket potatoes, a good choice of ploughman's and several Dorset 'Doorstep' sandwiches. Starters include fresh garlic mushrooms on toast and a combo starter for two - potato skins, Cajun coated onion rings and Japanese style breaded prawns followed by sizzling steaks, home-made steak and kidney pie smoked haddock pasta, lamb balti, home cooked ham and eggs, salmon and broccoli mornay and an 8 ounce Cumberland sausage served with potatoes, vegetables and onion gravy. For vegetarians there are meals like mushroom and nut fettucine and vegetable lasagne verdi. Sweets range from home-made banoffi and apple pie to toffee ice-cream sundae and Misty Irish Morn liqueur ice-cream.

The inn is open all day from 11 - 11. Sunday 12 noon - 10.30.

Children welcome in pub, dogs in the garden only.

Telephone: (01305) 889361. Fax: (01305) 889531.

"Triple-ramparted Maiden gloomed grayly"
My Cicely

Biographical Notes:
A favourite walk of Hardy's and the cause of dispute between Hardy and
Edward Cunnington, a local antiquary; the subject of the short story "A Tryst at
an Ancient Earthwork", published in the Detroit Post on March 1885 and in
England in December 1893. He referred to Cunnington in a paper he read at a
Dorchester meeting of the Field Club on 13 May 1884. Perhaps because of fear
of libel, the paper was mysteriously omitted from the published 'Proceedings'
for 6 years. It dealt with the discovery of skeletons, urns, and other
Roman/British relics found during digging of the foundations of his house at
Max Gate. Cunnington had made a number of archaeological finds near
Dorchester, including an amber cup 'allegedly complete until Cunnington trod
on it'. Richard Purdy has in his private collection a dried bunch of flowers once
belonging to Hardy with a date of 25 September 1910 and the words 'Maiden
Castle' attached, a memento of some romantic occasion, perhaps with Florence,
later to become the second Mrs. Hardy?

In July 1921 Hardy drove out to Maiden Castle with a company of film actors in
the course of making 'THE MAYOR OF CASTERBRIDGE'. They started out
from the King's Arms and Hardy was most amused to observe that although the
actors were fully made up and wore the costume of some 80 years earlier, the
townsfolk of Dorchester took absolutely no notice.

Literary Associations:
'My Cicely' - a poem about an old lover who traversed "The Ancient West
Highway", the old Roman road from London to Exeter, in search of his lost love.
He passes through Dorchester (Casterbridge) in sight of "triple-ramparted
Maidon", passing the earthworks and Eggardon and Poundbury (Square
Pummerie). "After The Club Dance", "The Alarm", "Mai-Don" are other poems
written around this spot. "Black'on frowns east on Maidon" (Blackdown over-
looks Maiden Castle) and from the Hardy monument the best view of the earth-
work is found, with every ridge and ditch visible, as Hardy points out in THE
DYNASTS.

Historical Interest:
The original name was Mai-Dun (the hill of strength). This stupendous earth
works encloses approximately 45 acres in the inner area and 115 acres overall.
It was the stronghold of the Durotriges and possibly identifiable as the Dunium
of Ptolemy. It was constructed throughout a series of occupations, the earliest
probably circa 2,000 BC, and like Eggardon Camp it is moulded to the hill. It is
a perfect example of a surviving Iron Age camp or fort. Settlers, however, have
left their mark here since Neolithic times but the causeway camp of this period
has been virtually destroyed.

The Walk:

Martinstown is signed from the Monkey Jump roundabout at the western end of the A35 Dorchester by-pass.

Park in the road at the front or in the large car park to the left and rear of the pub.

Approximate distance: 5¾ miles. OS Map 194 SY 643/890.

A very enjoyable scenic walk from this lovely Dorset village which takes you across farm land and high up Hog Hill beside Maiden Castle - an Iron Age hill fort which features in the MAYOR OF CASTERBRIDGE. The undulating terrain is almost entirely on bridleways making it suitable for mountain bike riders.

1. From the pub turn left into Burnside crossing over before reaching the church, cross the little bridge and join the footpath opposite, signposted Greathill 1¾. Follow the farm road up the hillside taking time to look back and enjoy the view, pass through the gate keeping to the well beaten field path across to the gate and out to the track. Two gates later join the track southwards and after climbing steadily through a series of farm gates turn left upon reaching the fingerpost.

2. From this inland section of the Dorset Coast Path there are far

Maiden Castle

reaching views south across Weymouth and Portland. After passing several tumuli fork left, go through the gate and further on bear half left walking across the field in the direction of the fingerpost signposted, bridleway to Martinstown. Pass through the gate into the field and bear half-left across to the gate in the far corner. Turn left, enter the field ahead and bear right down to the distant gate. Pass through the farmyard and go between the cottages turning left upon reaching the road.

3. Keeping to the right-hand side of the road walk 50 paces turning into the lane on the right towards Winterbourne Monkton. Keep straight ahead at the crossroads and after crossing the bridge enter the field on the left signposted, bridleway to Dorchester. Near the top a stile allows access to explore the fort.

4. Keep straight ahead through a couple of gates then turn left at the bridleway signposted, to Monkey's Jump. Turn left at the cross track signposted, to Martinstown, enter the farmyard, turning left then right bearing right to rejoin the track which passes between farm buildings before eventually reaching the road.

5. Carefully cross over into Bat Lane and join the signed bridleway leading to the farm (cyclists turn left) then follow the footpath ahead behind the church where a stone stile allows access through the church yard to the road retracing your steps back to the pub.

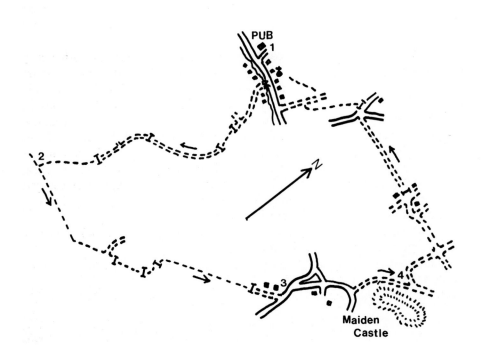

MELBURY
OSMOND
(Great Hintock)
(King's Hintock)
EVERSHOT
(Evershead)

The Acorn Hotel
Evershot

Peacefully tucked away in remotest Dorset is the beautiful unspoilt village of Evershot. It has inspired many not least Thomas Hardy who referred to the village as Evershead in TESS OF THE D'URBERVILLES. Centered in the main street is the Acorn. Dating from the 16th century the main bar, heated by an open log fire set in a stone fireplace, is simply furnished with old flintlocks and stuffed birds on the walls. There is a small bar at the back with its own entrance, a separate beamed candlelit restaurant and a few picnic benches in the small rear garden.

Being a real ale enthusiast I am always impressed with the range on offer. During my last visit I had the choice between Goldfinch Midnight Blinder, Munrows Mickey Finn, Fullers London Pride, Berkeley Lord's Prayer and Ringwood Old Thumper plus an excellent wine list.

Superb food, all freshly prepared, beautifully presented and efficiently served is available daily from 12 noon and up to 9.30 in the evening. Apart from the usual snacks of sandwiches and ploughman's the daily specials board might list tasty home-made soup, venison, marinated herrings in Madeira, smoked meat platter, pigeon breast a la garlic and Madeira sauce, garlic mushrooms, game casserole, home-made steak and kidney pie, fresh fish parcels, cauliflower cheese, chicken curry, peppered beef - juilenne of beef and peppers, stir fried vegetables, Thai prawns sizzler and sizzling duck with peach and ginger. Children and vegetarians are equally catered for, as are sweet lovers who can choose between lemon zing trifle or hot toffee pancake with ice cream to name but two.

Overnight accommodation is available with a choice of four poster beds.

Dogs and families are equally welcome.

Opening times are from 11.30 - 2.30 (Saturday 3 p.m.) and 6.30 - 11 Sunday 12 noon - 3 & 7 - 10.30.

Telephone: (01935) 83228.

*"Hintock House appeared immediately beneath her eye.
To describe it as standing in a hollow would not express
the situation of the manor-house; it stood in a hole.
But the hole was full of beauty."*
                    THE WOODLANDERS

Biographical Notes:
Townsend, Melbury Osmond was the home of Hardy's maternal ancestors. His mother, Jemima, was baptised and married in the Church of St Osmond; her marriage certificate dated 1839 hangs framed on the wall of the church. His grandmother, Elizabeth Hand, nee Swetman, lived here as a girl. His novel, THE WOODLANDERS is the first novel in which he makes clear that the countryside of Hardy's Wessex is not a real place but an inventive picture drawing upon its creator's memories of a real place. The exact Wessex of the books exists nowhere outside them.

Literary Associations:
The Hintocks are the most elusive of Hardy's situations. In 1926 Hardy wrote to a correspondent; "You will be surprised and shocked at my saying that I myself do not know where "Little Hintock" is! Several tourists have told me that they have found it, in every detail, and have offered to take me to it, but I have never gone....it has features which were to be found fifty years ago in the hamlets of Hermitage, Middlemarsh, Lyons-Gate, Revels Inn, Holnest, Melbury Bubb, etc..." In later editions he appears to have tried to shift the location eastwards. He was apparently anxious that the dubious Mrs Charmond of THE WOODLANDERS, living at Hintock House, should not be confused with any member of the Ilchester family. Therefore the description of the fictional house more closely resembles Turnworth House, which no longer exists. In fact he did seriously annoy the Ilchester family with his short story the "First Countess of Wessex", in which King's-Hintock Court was identified as the Ilchester family seat. Tess of the d'Urbervilles passes King's Hintock estates briefly with Angel Clare but the district is best known for the setting of THE WOODLANDERS, the novel Hardy is said to have considered his best. It was a part of the country he loved the best. Barber Percomb travelling from Sherborne (Sherton) on the carrier going to Cerne Abbas (Abbot's Cernel) is looking for Little Hintock; "'tis such a little small place that, as a town gentleman you'd need have a candle and lantern to find it...." he was told. The directions given to him suggest the hamlet of Hermitage. However, the scene where Tim and Suke were going with the wedding party suggest Revels Farm, which was once a posting house at Middlemarsh. Fitzpiers and Grace climbed the serpentine road ascending out of Lyon's Gate village. The site of Great Hintock House would appear to be Melbury Sampford (which was the seat of the Earl of Ilchester) but not the description of the house. The Cross-in-Hand, or Crossy Hand was the motif for

the poem "The Lost Pyx". A short story "The Dukes Reappearance" is set in Melbury Osmond.

Historical Interest:
The Swetman family is supposed to have been concerned in the Monmouth Rebellion. There is no Swetman named in those executed but it is possible that a Hardy ancestor was transported for his involvement in the cause. Hardy believed that this contributed to the "ruin" of the yeoman farming land, which was later absorbed into the estates of the Earls of Ilchester. The land had been theirs, according to Hardy "when the Ilchesters were at plow".

The Walk:

Evershot is signed from the A37 at Holywell north of Dorchester.

Approximate distance: 6½ miles. OS Map 194 ST 573/045.

Ample parking at the front of the inn or in the rear car park.

This very scenic and fairly long walk, starting from Evershot one of many lovely villages set deep in this peaceful part of West Dorset, guides you first through the beautiful Melbury Park Estate, then through pretty Melbury Osmond (Thomas Hardy's Great Hintock) before reaching the Lewcombe Estate finally returning on field paths. Although generally good underfoot a few areas can become very muddy and challenging in places.

1. Turn left from the inn walking down to the green at the road junction. The standing stones now built into a seat are, according to Peter Knight in his book, Ancient Stones of Dorset, believed to represent the three dumb sisters. Turn left here and enter the Melbury Estate. Cross the stile beside the cattle grid and continue through the park keeping straight ahead at the fork, through the metal gate and into the deer enclosure. There are usually plenty to be seen grazing on the surrounding lawns. Pass through a second gate and when level with the house, turn left following the tarred drive ahead, through several gates before reaching the stile on the far side. A seat has been provided in the enclosure to rest awhile.

2. Turn right following the lane into the pretty and peaceful village of Melbury Osmond, crossing the bridge and turning left into the lane opposite Rock Cottage. The tarred surface soon narrows to a grass track leading to a farm gate. Keep going over a track and up to a pair of metal farm gates. Follow the gravel track ahead which dips between a woodland strip, across a bridge rising to a wooden gate. At the end of the track pass through the metal gate and keeping close to the hedge walk down to the bottom turning right and almost immediately pass through the small metal gate on the left. Often muddy

and very uneven the narrow path drops steeply down through trees to a bridge. Go through the gate keeping straight ahead, across the grass and up the bank to the small metal gate opposite. Keeping close to the hedge walk up the field making for the wide metal gate in the top corner. The attractive, rather lumpy and often muddy path beyond rises steadily past attractive woodland finally reaching the road at the top.

3. Turn left, walk for awhile then turn left through the gateway of Lewcombe Manor (there is a gate to the left of the cattle grid). Carry on down the tarred drive, through the gate beside the cattle grid and, after passing the cottage climb the stile into the field on the right. Cross in the direction of the waymark heading for the gate in the opposite hedge

(presently green) then bear right down to the stile in the far right-hand corner. Go down the bank to the stream, carefully cross and climb the steep bank to the crossing point opposite.

4. Keep straight ahead in the field gradually drawing nearer to the hedge on the left. Upon reaching the far hedge pass through the gate into the field ahead and make for the gate opposite bearing right in the field, up to the metal farm gate and through onto the track. Just before reaching Girt Farm, climb the stile into the field on the left walking behind the buildings and out through the gate turning left onto the tarred drive. Climbing steeply take time to look back and enjoy the glorious Dorset scenery. Bear right at the top walking until you reach the stile on the left.

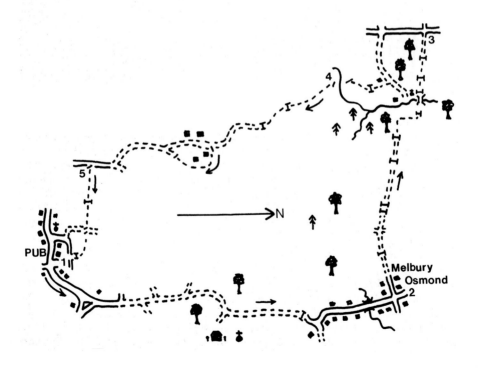

5. Climb into the field and go down to the far hedge where there are two gates. Enter the field on the left, walk down to the stile, over the track and stile and into the field ahead. Bearing right make your way down to the bottom right-hand corner and just before reaching the dwelling turn right at the boundary hedge, pass through the gate, go down to the lane and turn left. A short distance ahead look for a narrow path on the right which leads straight to the rear car park of the pub.

Melbury Osmond

Melbury Park

Walk No. 10

OWERMOIGNE
(Nether Moynton)
& MORETON
(Moreford Rise)

The Countryman Inn
East Knighton

Away from the main road down a short gravel track is the delightful Countryman Inn. Originally known as The Rising Sun the inn has benefited from careful refurbishment retaining and improving the delightful rustic atmosphere. The front entrance leads directly into the old pub; two lovely cosy rooms each with an open fire and the main bar beyond. Bare brick walls are much in evidence with lots of comfortable farmhouse chairs and padded parlour chairs. There is a comfortable games room, a family room and restaurant. Picnic benches are neatly positioned on the front lawn with further seating and a kiddies play area at the back.

The inn is family pub extremely well run by the owners Jeremy and Nina Evans. The well stocked bar includes a well balanced and interesting wine list and a good choice of real ales which presently include Wadworth 6X, Directors Bitter, Courage Best, Old Speckled Hen and two Ringwood brews their Best Bitter and Old Thumper.

Very good home cooked food is available every day from 12 noon - 2 and 6.30 - 9.30. All food is freshly prepared and delays may occur at busy times. Apart from the usual snacks like home-made soup, ploughman's, sandwiches and filled rolls the set menu lists a range of appetiser's including hot garlic stuffed mushrooms followed by filled fillet of plaice and lemon sole, pan fried sardines and butterfly prawns. Also listed are various grills and a good choice for vegetarians like tomato & lentil lasagne and penne pasta in a rich tomato and herb sauce with a cheese and chive topping. There is comprehensive kiddie's menu, a good sweet list, a carvery plus daily specials which might include traditional steak and kidney pie, duck breast served with orange and braised steak in red wine and mushrooms.

Six en suite bedrooms, singles, double and family rooms
Opening times 11 - 3 and 6 - 11 Sunday 12 noon - 3 and 6 - 10.30.
Children and dogs equally welcome.
Telephone: (01305) 852666. Fax: (01305) 854125.

'Not smugglers' liquor?' he said.
'Yes' said she. 'They are tubs of spirit that have accidentally
floated over in the dark from France'
                                    The Distracted Preacher

Biographical Notes:
John Hardy of Puddletown (1755-1821) Thomas Hardy's great-grandfather is
assumed to be the son of John Hardy of Owermoigne and his wife, Elizabeth
Swire, who were married in 1746. Elizabeth Swire is probably the ancestor of
pure Irish descent (as Hardy once described her in a letter to Lady Gregory) and
her husband the sea-going Hardy who bequeathed his telescope to his son and
then down through the family to Hardy's father and ultimately to his brother
Henry.

Hardy's father evidently did some building work in Owermoigne. In 1911, a
farmer in the village was able to point out the cottage where "Mr Hardy's father
used to lodge as a young man, when he was engaged on the building of Galton
farmhouse nearby".

The connection with Moreton is through Hardy's friendship with T E Lawrence
(the former Lawrence of Arabia). Lawrence was then serving as Private Shaw
in the army camp at Bovington. He asked Robert Graves for an introduction to
the author. Liking and admiration on both sides was instantaneous and
Lawrence visited Max Gate frequently when his duties allowed. Florence
Hardy even persuaded him to let her ride in his motorcycle sidecar. Lawrence
said of Hardy: "They used to call this man a pessimist. While really he is full of
fancy expectations." Lawrence is buried in Moreton churchyard.

Literary Associations:
Moreford Rise has a passing mention in Hardy's poem "The Slow Nature", it is a
hill close to Moreton. In "THE RETURN OF THE NATIVE", a turning to the
left from Moreton North Lodge, bearing to the left again, led to the cottage
Clym rented after his marriage to Eustacia, called Alderworth: "it was almost as
lonely as that of Eustacia's grandfather, but the fact that it stood near to heath
was disguised by a belt of firs which almost enclosed the premises."

In April 1879 one of Hardy's best short stories was published in the New
Quarterly Magazine. "The Distracted Preacher" is set in Owermoigne and is
based largely on stories he heard from George Nicholls, formerly a coast guard
at Kimmeridge and the father of Eliza, a girl Hardy was once involved with.
Other sources were Captain Masters, his landlord at Swanage, and the experi-
ences of his own grandparents. His grandfather at the Bockhampton cottage
would be wakened by a whiplash against the window in the dead of night and
come downstairs to find a heap of tubs outside his front door. These were
secreted in a cupboard, but, as Hardy relates, the 100% proof spirit was so
strong the smell pervaded the cottage. Owermoigne was a common smugglers'

haunt only three miles from the coast with unpopulated downland in between. The Gothic church was rebuilt in 1883 (after the date of the story). The stairs to the "singing gallery" are no more but the tower where the smugglers lay hidden on the roof is still there. Lizzie Newberry's house was between the village cross and the mill, opposite the rectory in Church Lane. The orchard belonging to the smuggler, Jim Owlett, however, does not actually join the cottage garden but lies a short distance away, where the "cave" in which the tubs were hidden left a depression in the ground. The forge where the sabotaged carts were repaired, very slowly, by the village blacksmith for the Customs-men is now a private residence on the corner of Holland's Mead Avenue.

The preacher, a young Methodist sent to the village as a locum before a permanent appointment was made, lodged with Lizzie Newberry, a young widow, and fell in love with her. Inevitably he became involved with her smuggling activities but begged her to give it up. She is reluctant, she needs the money and enjoys the excitement. He follows her at night, crossing the high road, climbing the steep hill towards Ringstead Bay (Ringworth), and passing the "lonely hamlet of Holworth" where the sound of the sea could soon be heard. On the next more successful expedition, they walk to Dagger's Cove, near Lulworth (Lulwind) via Lord's Barrow and Chaldon (Shaldon) Down. The Customs men find this cargo after searching the village and set off to Weymouth (Budmouth). At Warmwell (Warm'ell Cross) they are ambushed by the smugglers and tied to nearby trees. But the offer of a good reward for the smugglers' capture "dead or alive" kills off the trade in Nether Moynton. The miller emigrates and in the story Lizzie marries the Methodist preacher, repenting her former life and using her experience to write religious tracts preaching "Render unto Caesar..."

Historical Notes:
Owermoigne - the village has a history of contraband trade. In 1849, the Rev. S Osborne wrote "Smuggling gave a very large amount of employment to the peasantry of the country, and, directly and indirectly, put a great deal of money in their way." The Church of St Michael was factually involved and possibly the rectory also, where a bricked up window is thought to be the receiving point for illicit tubs of spirits. The Elizabethan rectory has beams inside taken from a vessel of the Spanish Armada wrecked in Ringstead Bay.

Smuggling was widely accepted by all walks of life at the time, the general attitude best expressed by the words of Lizzie Newberry: "Why should you side with men who take from country traders what they have honestly bought wi' their own money in France?"

In a preface, Hardy says "I might add that the action of this story is founded on certain smuggling exploits that occurred between 1825 and 1830, and were brought to a close in the latter year by the trial of the chief actors at the Assizes before Baron Bolland for their desperate armed resistance to the Custom-house officers during the landing of a cargo of spirits." In May 1912, he added a note to the effect that the conventional ending was "de rigueur" at the time of writing. The truth was that Lizzie stuck by Jim the smuggler and emigrated with him to America. They both died in Wisconsin between 1850 and 1860.

Moreton - T E Lawrence was killed in a motor cycle accident near his home at Clouds Hill, where Mr & Mrs Hardy and E M Forster were once treated to a "sumptuous tea". His funeral on May 21 1935 was attended by many notable figures including the Rt Hon Winston Churchill and his wife, Bernard Shaw, Augustus John, General Wavell and others.

St Nicholas Church is well known for its long association with the Frampton family of Dorset. It was rebuilt twice and enlarged by the family. On October 8 1940 the building suffered severe damage caused by a stray bomb which fell in the churchyard. After the war, repairs were completed in 1950. Today the church is famous for its unique windows of engraved glass, the work of Laurence Whistler, on the theme of Light both physical and spiritual.

Moreton House appears in the Seasons Window in the north aisle, depicted in a snowstorm. Murray's Handbook of 1882 describes it as a "plain stone mansion", containing interesting portraits of Charles I and Henrietta Maria; the ill-fated Duchess of Orleans; Lady Jane Grey and Tregonwell Frampton, keeper of the royal race-horses at Newmarket to William III, etc. At that time the mansion had been in the hands of the Frampton family since 1365, in the reign of Edward III.

(St Martin's Church, Wareham, has a fine effigy of T E Lawrence in Arabian dress, by Eric Kennington, who also sculpted Thomas Hardy's statue at the top of the town, Dorchester.)

Moreton House

Walk No. 10

The Walk:

Pub signed just west of Wool off the A352 Dorchester road.

Approximate distance: 9½ miles. OS Map 194 SY 812/857.

There are large car parks at the front and back plus ample parking in the lane.

A long but enjoyable walk along peaceful Dorset lanes and bridle tracks. Starting from East Knighton field paths take you through the attractive village of Winfrith Newburgh and up a ridge passing Five Marys and Lord's Barrow before descending to Owermoigne. After reaching Redbridge an optional route north along country lanes will take you to Moreton passing Moreton House and the cemetery where T E. Lawrence is buried. Otherwise your route back is south across Winfrith Heath.

1. Walk back up to the main road cross over turning left and join the footpath between the dwellings signposted, to School Lane. After a series of stiles turn right into the lane. Cross at the road junction, go down the track to the bridge and turn left along the riverside path.

2. Exit into the road and turn right and soon afterwards turn right into the entrance to Winards Farm. Turn left at the top, bridleway signposted, to Five Marys. Follow the field path, which rises steadily, up-hill beside the hedge (lovely views north across Winfrith Heath). Enter the field at the top and keep straight ahead past the tumuli to the road and continue ahead to the gate. Maintain your direction through more gates, then cross the road through a series of gates eventually turning right into the lane. After a nice gradual descent carefully cross the busy main road into Owermoigne one of Dorset's nicest villages.

3. The lane is long but fairly peaceful with several attractive dwellings and small garden centres one of which houses a cider museum and a collection of Dorset clocks. Open from 9 a.m. - 5 p.m. Cross the road bridge and continue along the lane. On the right is a signed bridleway either follow this route to the lane and turn left up to Redbridge or keep to the lane and take the next right at the top of the hill signposted, to Moreton then right into the road.

4. Cross the railway bridge and unless you want to keep to the lane to Moreton passing Moreton House and the grave of T E Lawrence turn immediately right along the un-made county road following this track for 1¼ miles turning right into the lane at Broomhill Bridge. At the next turning on the right climb the hill onto Winfrith Heath walking as far as the entrance to Winfrith. At the boundary gates turn right along the fence go up and round to the left then down and away from the fence turning left onto the narrow track leading to the rear of the pub.

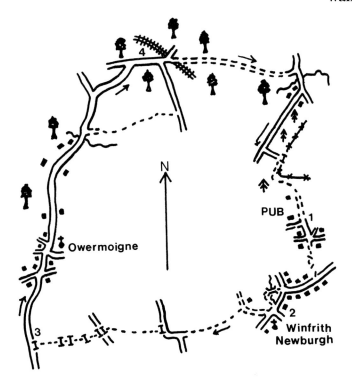

The Gothic church, Owermoigne

Walk No. 11

PORTLAND
(Isle of Slingers)

The Pulpit Inn

Portland was no doubt once an island but is now linked to the mainland by the spectacular Chesil Beach. It is a rugged block of limestone about 4 miles long and 2 miles wide rising at its highest point to 496 feet above the sea. The Island is unique often experiencing different weather than that of the mainland.

Deriving its name from the Pulpit Rock, a precarious stack on the point by the lighthouse, this solid pub built from local stone occupies a sunny position overlooking the sea on the Bill of Portland. Heated by an open fire the mostly open plan interior is carpeted and comfortably furnished and there is a separate large dining/function room. Picnic benches are neatly positioned on the two front terraces maximising the lovely view.

Well run by the licensee Danny Fox the bar presently includes at least two real ales Salisbury Best Bitter and The Bishop's Tipple.

Food available all week from 12 noon - 3 and 7 - 10 (9.30 Sunday) is ordered from a separate servery with daily fresh fish specials supplementing the main menu. Apart from the usual snacks like home-made soup, ploughman' and sandwiches, hot dishes include home-made steak and kidney pie, beef curry, ham and eggs and a choice of home-made pizzas. There is separate children's choice and a very good vegetarian selection listing 5 starters followed by 6 main courses like leek & Stilton bake and broccoli & cream cheese bake. A more comprehensive menu is available in the evening which includes dishes such as Portland crab salad, fresh lemon sole, half a honey roast duck and a sizzling skillet special - slices of fillet steak or chicken breasts marinated with peppers and onions. Fresh lobster is available to order.

Children and dogs equally welcome.

B & B for 3 doubles and 1 single.

Weekday opening times 11 30 - 3 and 7 - 11.30 Sunday 12 noon - 2.30 and 7 - 9.30.

Telephone: (01305) 821237.

"Stretches out like the head of a bird into the English Channel"
THE WELL-BELOVED

Biographical Notes:
Portland fascinated Hardy and he paid many visits to the island. When he and
Emma were staying in Swanage they heard many tales of smuggling, one of
which concerned a fishing boat going to meet a French lugger to take off contraband. They were seen by the revenue cutter so they snapped the ends off
their clay pipes and pretended to use them as bait for fishing. The ruse worked
and they even caught some mackerel with this 'bait'. He also learned that when
persons are drowned in West Bay or 'Deadman's Bay' just to the west of Portland
"the sea undresses them".

In February 1879 Hardy talked to a woman who told about the great storm of
1824. The ruined walls in Lower Chesil were all that remained of a house that
was washed down in the November gale. The owner never rebuilt it. She said in
her own house one person was drowned, they were all in bed except the fisher-
men, and next door two people. Many also died that night.

In 1890 Sir George Douglas came to stay at Max Gate. Hardy took him to
Portland where they lunched at The Mermaid, Wakeham.

In July 1900, when he was sixty, he cycled with a friend to Portland Bill and
back to Max Gate.

In 1923 Hardy was invited by Admiral Fisher on board a battleship. Florence
Hardy recalls that in old age Hardy loved to walk 'the triangle' from Max Gate.
He loved standing by the railway line watching the goods trucks laden with
Portland stone passing by. "He said he thought that the shape of Portland would
be changed in the course of years by the continual cutting away of its surface."

Friendship with Marie Stopes, the pioneer of birth control, led Florence to con-
fess her inability to 'enter into the love-making' described in Marie Stopes' novel
'Love's Creation', and she appears to have consulted her about their inability to
conceive, probably without Hardy's knowledge. A letter from her dated 5th
September 1923 says "I find in talking to him that the idea of my having a child
at his age fills him with horror......"

Literary Associations:
Principally THE WELL-BELOVED is centred in Portland, interspersed with
scenes in London society, for which he appeared to be making notes during the
London season of 1887. The serial was published from 1st October to 17
December 1892. Hardy describes it as 'a bygone, wildly romantic fancy' but to

outsiders it looked like a comment on marriage and, by implication, on his own unsatisfactory marriage. When the story appeared in novel form, not until 1897, it was considerably toned down.

Avice Caro's cottage is now used as a museum, it was given to Portland for that purpose by Marie Stopes. It is a thatched building built in 1640. Pennsylvania Castle lies opposite. Pierston, the hero, climbs up Fortunswell (the Street of Wells) towards Eastern village (Easton). He visits the old graveyard at Church Ope Cove, headstones remain there though most of the church has gone. At the top is Rufus Castle or Bow-And-Arrow Castle (Red King's Castle). Pennsylvania Castle (Sylvania Castle) is the fictional residence of Marcia Bencombe. When he walks to Weymouth, Pierston crosses ferry-bridge, by now in situ. He shelters in the ruins of Sandsfoot Castle on the way to Weymouth (Budmouth).

Portland also comes into the story of THE TRUMPET MAJOR. Bob the sailor is fond of the sea and enjoys watching the activities of the harbour. Ann goes out to Portland Bill to watch him sail away in the Victory with Nelson.

Historical Interest:
Pebbles were used as slingshot by prehistoric man - which probably suggested Hardy's name for the Island (the Isle of Slingers).

The Fleet, the stretch of water cut off by the shingle beach between Portland and Abbotsbury, was much used by smugglers and is the setting for Faulkner's 'MOONFLEET'.

Wooden viaducts across Weymouth backwater and the Fleet brought the railway to Portland in the mid 1860's. The wood was later replaced with iron. The line was closed in 1965.

Portland Castle, like Sandsfoot Castle on the Weymouth side, were built on Henry VIII's instructions to defend the harbour. So it is fitting that the name Avice derives from Avice Talbot, the daughter of the Talbots who owned Talbothays land in the time of Henry VIII. This land much later came into possession of the Hardy family, where Thomas built a house for his brother Henry and his sisters to live in.

Pennsylvania Castle was built in 1800 for John Penn, grandson of William Penn founder of Pennsylvania, U.S.A. and once the governor of Portland. Below the castle steep steps lead down to the remains of St Andrews, the oldest church on the Island and the parish church until 1756.

The white sea-mark on the edge of the Bill with initials TH belongs to Trinity House.

Avice Caro's cottage

Rufus Castle

Walk No. 11

Rufus Castle, the oldest building on the island is a medieval ruin.

St. Peter's church was built by convict labour in 1872 and decorated with a mosaic pavement laid by Constance Kent, a convicted murderess, sentenced to life imprisonment and released in 1885.

St. Andrews at Southwell was built by subscription from friends and relatives of those lost at sea in the collision between two ships, the Avalanche and the Forest.

St. George, Reforne, built in 1777 of fine Portland ashlar, "among a fantasy of monuments" was where Pierston attended Avice's funeral.

The Walk:

Portland, best reached from the A354 south of Dorchester, is a migration stop for many birds over 300 having been recorded it is also home to 30 species of butterflies and some 720 species of moths. The Inn is situated at the southern most tip at the Bill of Portland.

Approximate distance: 5¼ miles. OS Map 194 677/687.

Large car park at front of pub and public car park near the lighthouse.

Wild flowers and butterflies abound all the way along this extremely enjoyable scenic coastal walk which guides you, precariously in places, around the southern half of Portland passing by the remains of St Andrews Church, Avice Caro's cottage, the ruins of Rufus Castle - the oldest building on the Island and Pennsylvania Castle. The coast path can be a little demanding in places but negotiable with care. Try and walk in spring or summer preferably on a warm sunny day.

1. From the pub walk down to the lighthouse and turn left along the coast path passing at first between the beach huts. It is easy to follow needing little or no explanation and the scenery is stunning with numerous wild flowers and butterflies. Marbled whites and common blues can be seen flying around large swathes of red valerian which grows alongside blue viper's bugloss and yellow samphire. Undulating in places the path threads its way through several disused quarries before eventually rising to the road.

2. Turn right and a short distance later turn right into the view point at Cheyne Weare where picnic benches and information boards are provided. During spring and summer migrating birds can often be seen flying in the area. Continue north along the nar-

row coastal path, which can be precarious in places. Although not too hard to follow try and keep to the path nearest to the cliff edge, where you will find some stone steps and the occasional yellow arrows to guide you. Upon reaching Church Ope Cove climb the short distance up the steps on the left if you wish to see the tombstones and derelict church otherwise climb the steps on the right and follow the tarred drive under the arch, past the café and Avice Caro's cottage, (now a museum) and out to the road.

3. Turn right, cross over and join the signed footpath on the left beside the disused railway line. Turn left through the quarry then right passing round the gate and follow the track ahead. Further on turn right, walk up to the dwellings and turn left. Keep to the path behind the houses, which eventually reaches the Weston Road.

4. Keep straight ahead beside the green and almost opposite the turning on the left cross the road and join the signed footpath opposite leading to the cliff edge. Wild flowers abound along this particularly attractive path, which hugs the cliff top heading south. After passing the MOD buildings on the left take the path on the

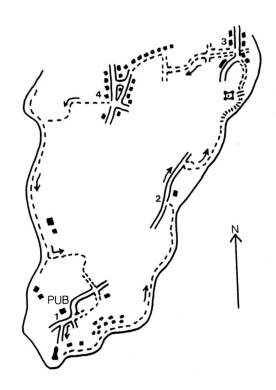

left signposted, East Cliff. Walk all around the edge of the field and down the track to the road turning right. After passing the field study centre take the path on the left then go right beside the quarry, a good place to observe birds and keep to the track past the dwellings back to the pub.

PUDDLETOWN
(Weatherbury)

The Prince of Wales
Puddletown

This homely roadside village inn has two bars the public with games and the comfortable lounge. Divided by a wrought iron screen the lounge bar has brown leatherette padded chairs and padded wooden benches, the bar is of herringbone brick construction and there is a brick fireplace at one end. Early photographs of the village are displayed on the walls together with a notice stating that the skittle alley was used as a billet by service personal prior to D Day and used afterwards by the 18th American Infantry Regiment. There are picnic benches on the forecourt with more on the rear lawn where there is also a children's play area.

Owned by Hall & Woodhouse the inn is well run by the tenants. In addition to reasonably wines there are two real ales, Badger Best and Tanglefoot.

Bar snacks on the menu served every day of the week include soup, ploughman's and sandwiches plain and toasted with fillings such as ham with pineapple. Daily blackboard specials might include breaded scampi, steak and Murphy's pie, battered cod, lasagne, Mississippi chicken breast and the very popular honey roast ham, egg and chips. Also listed pasta fromaggio made with chicken and ham, broccoli and cream cheese bake, garlic mushrooms, macaroni cheese, various steaks and butterfly chicken with garlic and herbs. There is a separate children's menu. Sweets range from home-made Dorset apple cake to fruit pies.

Children welcome, well behaved dogs in public bar only

Weekday opening times 11 - 3 and 6.30 - 11. Sunday 12 noon - 3 and 7 - 10 30.

Telephone: (01305) 848222.

"Moreover, the Weatherbury folk were by no means uninteresting intrinsically. If report spoke truly they were as hardy, merry, thriving, wicked a set as any in the whole county."
Far From The Madding Crowd

Biographical Notes:

Hardy's more disreputable relations, mainly the Hands and Sparks, related to his mother, lived at Puddletown. Jemima Hardy's sister Mary was married to the shoemaker there, John Antell, and when he beat his wife, Jemima and her other sisters cornered John Antell and retaliated in force. John Antell's history bears a certain resemblance to JUDE THE OBSCURE and Hardy was far from being an enemy to the man. When living in Wimborne, Hardy wrote a most cordial letter to Antell's son, also John, who had a local reputation as a poet, concerning the design of a headstone for the shoemaker's grave. The son evidently thought well enough of Hardy to send him sketches and ask for his advice.

Hardy's cousin Tryphena Sparks is rumoured to have been Hardy's lover and there is even a suggestion that she had his child, but this has been largely disproved recently. He did, however, give her a photograph of himself taken in 1862 when he was 22 and is said to have given her a ring at one time, but not necessarily an engagement ring.

Hardy was fond of taking guests from Max Gate to see Puddletown Church, where his grandfather played in the gallery. Sir Arthur Blomfield and Gustav Holst both climbed up into the gallery where Hardy's ancestors had sat. Although Hardy had a reputation for ignoring his Puddletown relatives, this is disproved by frequent visits paid by the Sparks cousins to Max Gate.

Literary Associations:

The village is much changed since the time in which FAR FROM THE MADDING CROWD is set and Hardy himself took considerable liberties with the topography of the place. Bathsheba's farm, for instance, is supposed to be on a hill to the west of the church "not more than a quarter of a mile" away. In reality, Waterston Manor, the house most closely resembling her farm is more than a mile away. Now a private house, it is recognisable from Hardy's description. Druce Farm nearby is said to be the original of Farmer Boldwood's residence. Puddletown Church is set upon a slight rise which Hardy exaggerated in the book but it does have gargoyles and the one on the south-east corner could have thrown a spout of water in a great "liquid parabola" as the author described. Behind the church where Fanny Robin's grave was screened from the passersby, there are several ancient yew trees. In the porch, which is the main entrance to the church, Sergeant Troy spent the night. Inside the church on an old box pew underneath the gallery is carved the name HENERY, a reminder of Henery Fray a rustic character from the same book who always wrote his name that way.

TESS OF THE D'URBERVILLES seems to permeate the Dorset countryside. Here she crops up again. From the top of a hill near Weatherbury she first saw her future home in the Vale of the Great Dairies. Tess and Angel drove through Weatherbury shortly before they parted.

Troytown (Roytown) the "road-side hamlet" nearby is where Joseph Poorgrass halted with Fanny Robin's coffin. The pub, The Bull's Head, has since been pulled down.

Historical Interest:
Hardy's remark, more than a century later, that the people of Puddletown were addicted to "fuddling" was probably very true in 1725 when there were six public houses in the village: King's Arms, Nagg's Head, The Boot, The Greyhound, The Five Bells and The White Lyon. Later there was a pub called The Old Cat whose dregs were deposited in the river. Hence the description of a typical Puddletown Sunday:-

> Into Church,
> Out of Church,
> Into Cat,
> Out of Cat,
> Into Piddle.

In medieval times the name was Piddleton, on the River Piddle. The Gemut or Hundred Court was held there. The ring in the middle of the church's south door is thought to be a Sanctuary ring for those fleeing from persecution or from the law. The shield at the centre of the front of the gallery carries the arms of England and France and is said to have been taken from a ship. Ancestors of the Martyn family of Athelhampton House are buried there and there are beautiful alabaster effigies of Martyn Knights.

Of interest in the churchyard there is a grave with a headstone of Peter Stanley, King of the Gypsies, who died November 23 1802. An altar tomb lies near the south path to the memory of William Amey, who raised a troop of Yeomen when Napoleon threatened England.

On August 8 1630 Winifred Turbervile was buried here.

Puddletown was once a much more important place. In 1860 there were 20 bootmakers, 12 blacksmiths, 20 carpenters and wheelwrights, five pairs of sawyers, two coopers and some cabinetmakers. The stocks and the court-house stood in the Square. Hardy's story FAR FROM THE MADDING CROWD is set in the 1840's and 1850's.

Walk No. 12

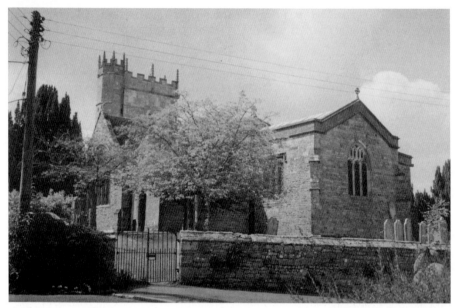

Puddletown Church

Bridleway at Castle Hill

The Walk:

Pub located on the main road in the centre of the village.

Approximate distance: 4½ miles. OS Map 194 ST 755/945.

Park either at the pub or in the lanes off the main road.

A very scenic walk in peaceful Dorset countryside which takes you south from Puddletown along attractive bridleways through Puddletown Forest then back through Ilsington Wood.

1. Turn right from the inn along the High Street, cross the road and just past Kings Mead join the path on the left. Walk up to the stile then climb the field to the top. Looking back one can see Druce Farm and beyond the Piddle Valley where Waterstone Manor lies. Cross the stile on the left and follow the path behind the school fence, climb the steps to the gate and keep straight ahead along the field boundary and out through the gate into the lane.

2. Walk straight across and join the signed bridleway opposite. Go as far as the buildings then pass through the gate into the field on the right and head to the gate at the top. Keep to the path through the wood then cross the track and, bearing right head up and over the field making for the metal farm gate. Follow the edge of the wood down and around the field until reaching the stile. Cross over into the adjoining field and walk up to the crossing point then con-

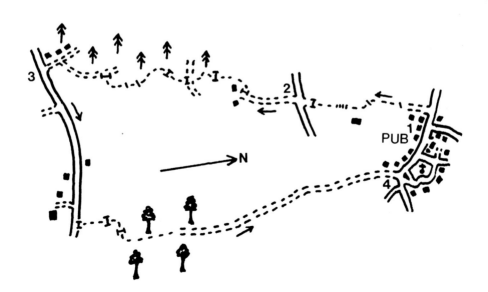

73

tinue down beside the woods until you reach a gate on the right. Climb over onto the narrow grass track and turn left. Attractively lined with blue-bells and pink campion it joins a wide gravel track down Castle Hill before reaching the road.

3. Turn left along this very attractive and peaceful lane walking for just over ½ a mile. Just beyond the entrance to Ilsington Farm House look for a small gate on the left (not the wide gate opposite the entrance) and walk up the field between the row of trees. Pass through the gate at the top walking round keeping as close as possible to the hedge on the right until you reach the small metal gate. The narrow path runs along the edge and through a section of Ilsington Wood attractively carpeted with bluebells. Pass a pond on the left and keep to the wide gravel track, which eventually meets the road at Puddletown.

4. Carefully cross the road into the lane opposite signed to Ilsington House. Pass the church and the entrance to Ilsington House. Circa 1690 the historic house and gardens are open to the public May through till September, Wednesdays and Thursdays afternoons from 2 p.m. - 6 p.m. August only Wednesday, Thursdays, Sundays and bank holi-day Mondays. Carry on through the Square and turn right then right at the road back to the pub.

Ilsington House

STURMINSTER
NEWTON
(Stourcastle)

The Bull Inn

A country feel pervades throughout this lovely old 15th century inn which nestles beneath the village of Broad Oak overlooking the Stour and the medieval six arched bridge built by John Selwood in the 16th century. Constructed from yellow ham stone, timber and brick under a partly thatched roof the main, low beamed bar has padded wall seats and simple farmhouse tables and chairs. One step down brings you into a cosy low beamed snug where there is a piano opposite the Victorian brick fireplace, a collection of books at one end and dressed walking sticks to purchase on show in a container beside the bar. There is separate skittle alley and beer garden.

Three real ales presently available in this well run and friendly Hall & Woodhouse tenancy are Tanglefoot, Dorset Best and IPA.

Generously portioned food is served from 12 noon - 2 and 7 - 9.30 (Sunday 9 p.m.) Apart from daily specials, which might include, twin chicken breasts in garlic, herbs, wine and brandy, rich venison casserole in red wine and secret herbs and a gammon special - generous slices in Dubonnet, cider and mustard sauce. Well portioned blackboard meals include smoked trout, soup, jacket potatoes, garlic bread, ploughman's and enormous filled baguettes, followed by various steaks, steak and Guinness, steak and mushroom with red wine, and chicken and mushroom in white wine, ham egg and chips, and chips with grated cheese. Also listed are Indian style beef or chicken Madras curries and a substantial all day breakfast. There is a selection of vegetarian meals and 2 course meals for young visitors. Sweet lovers can choose between home-made apple crumble and bread and butter pudding or maybe the Stilton in Port with biscuits.

Families and dogs welcome.

Weekday opening times 11.30 - 3 and 6 - 11 (6.30 Saturday) Sunday 12 noon - 3 and 7 - 10.30.

Telephone: (01258) 472435.

*"I had slowed along
After the torrid hours were done,
Though still the posts and walls and road
Flung back their sense of the hot-faced sun,
And had walked by Stourside Mill, where broad
Stream-lilies throng."*

The Musical Box

Biographical Notes:
After hints from their relatives that the Hardys "appeared to be wandering about like two tramps", they settled in Sturminster Newton. On July 3rd 1876 they moved into "Riverside Villa", after hastily furnishing it with £100 worth of Victorian furniture bought in two hours on an expedition to Bristol. It was their first house and the time spent there was very happy. "Rowed on the Stour in the evening, the sun setting up the river. Just afterwards a faint exhalation visible on the surface of water as we stirred it with the oars." He made many notes on local stories and legends. "Toad Fair" An old man, a wizard used to bring toads' legs in little bags to Bagber Bridge (close to his house) and sell them as charms to cure scrofula.

Riverside Villa, Sturminster Newton

June 28th being Coronation Day there are games and dancing on the green at Sturminster Newton..." (The 40th anniversary of her coronation)*.
*Queen Victoria

On the following day he makes a note about their servant Jane, who was found coming out of their outhouse with a man after midnight. Emma ordered her to bed and the man disappeared. Later they found out that Jane was soon to have a baby, Hardy adding the anguished note "Yet never a sign of one is there for us".

They lived there until 1878 when on March 18th, Hardy recorded. "End of the Sturminster idyll ... Our happiest time." He returned for brief visits several times, the last in 1922 when he was 81.

Literary Associations:
When living in Sturminster Newton he wrote THE RETURN OF THE NATIVE but used the background of Egdon Heath, twenty miles away. The town has a passing mention in TESS when the heroine drives through Stourcastle with her load of bee-hives for Dorchester. She parted from Angel Clare just outside the town, much later in the story, she travelling to Marlott and he to Beaminster, both returning to their parents' homes. The Colber Bridge inspired the poem "On Sturminster Foot-bridge" many years later, and "Overlooking The River Stour" and "The Musical Box" which are remembrances of Emma.

Historical Interest:
"Exceedingly ancient" according to Murray's Handbook for 1882. The town was bequeathed by Alfred to his son Ethelwold, and eventually appropriated by Glastonbury Abbey. At the Dissolution it was granted by Henry VIII to Katherine Parr and on her death, by Edward VI to Elizabeth. In the Civil War the Parliamentary forces had a garrison there which was forced by the Dorset Clubman (who fought against the troops on both sides). On July 3rd 1645 16 dragoons were taken prisoner and many killed and wounded.

Opposite the end of the bridge there is a moated mound on which a castle once stood, and fragments of building remain. One mile N.E. is Hinton St Mary where in 1963 excavation of a Roman villa revealed a magnificent tessellated pavement (now in the British Museum), bearing symbolism indicating the early presence of Christianity in this district circa 350 AD.

Walk No. 13

The Walk:

Pub located at Town Bridge on the A357.

Approximate distance: 6¼ miles. OS Map 194 ST 786/137.

Park in the lane at the side or in either of the two small car parks.

A very enjoyable walk beginning at Sturminster Mill which then follows a field path to reach Riverside Villa. After crossing the Stour the walk follows field paths, tracks and country lanes, passes beside Plumber Manor, crosses Okeford Common and skirts Banbury Hill before returning down an attractive peaceful country lane. Not over demanding the walk is generally good underfoot except for a few areas that can be very muddy in winter and late spring.

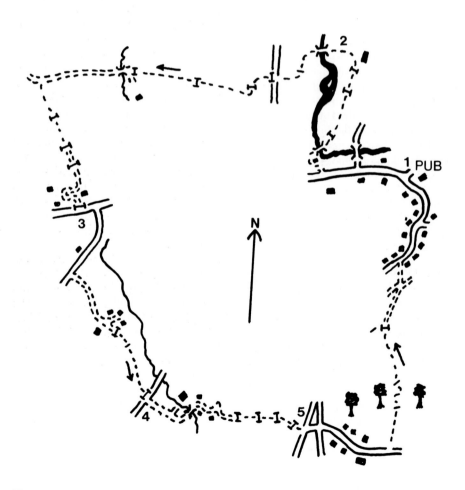

1. Leave the pub turning left, carefully cross the main road and in a short distance take the path signposted, to Sturminster Mill. Cross both bridges and pass through the kissing gate into the field following the well-beaten path towards the distant dwellings. Pass through the kissing gate at the top and cross the park to the gate opposite. Riverside Villa is on the right marked with a blue plaque.

2. Continue ahead close to the river turning left at the finger post, go over the bridge and bear left making for the stile in the far hedge. Follow the narrow track up to the lane and cross to the gate opposite. Bearing left make for the gate in the hedge, turn right in the field and walk to the stile at the top. Climb into the field ahead, leave by the gate at the bottom and keep straight ahead crossing the River Divelish following the track towards Woodland Farm. Ignore the stiles in the fence but keep walking as far as the finger post then pass through the gate into the field on the left and, bearing left head up the field to the gate, Pass into the field crossing diagonally left down to the gate at the bottom. Keep to the track up beside the hedge, through a couple of gates, bearing right then left between the farm buildings and out into the road.

3. Cross over turning left and almost immediately turn right into Puxey Lane. Undulating and peaceful the lane is home to many different wild flowers. Turn left upon reaching the bridleway signposted, to Plumber Manor. Keep straight ahead at Puxey Farm, through the farm gate, across the field to the small gate opposite and out through the large gate ahead.

4. Cross into the drive to Plumber Manor bearing right at the entrance gates following the track, over the bridge then up and round between the buildings to the gate. Walk up to the gate bearing right at the top then cross to one more gate, go out into the lane turning left.

5. Almost immediately cut across the narrow strip of land and join the lane ahead to Okeford Fitzpaine and Belchalwel. Follow the road for some distance, passed various dwellings and farm buildings. After climbing the rise enter the field on the left and, keeping close to the hedge walk to the stile at the bottom of the field. Follow the twisting path through the wood to the stile on the far side. Bearing left walk round Banbury Hill until you reach the gate then follow this attractive primrose and bluebell lined bridleway. If the route looks very muddy, and it can be in winter you have the option to follow the field path on the left.

6. Upon reaching the cross track and fingerpost signposted, Broad Oak ¼ keep straight ahead up another often muddy track turning right into the lane through the village of Broad Oak after which the route is all down hill back to the pub where seats are provided along the way for relaxation.

Walk No. 14

SUTTON
POYNTZ
& BINCOMBE
(Overcombe)

The Springhead
Sutton Poyntz

The charming little village of Sutton Poyntz once the home of local farm workers is one of the areas best kept secrets. The pure chalk spring which rises in the village is the source of Weymouth's water supply. Interestingly the filter in the reservoir is one of the funnels from Brunel's great steamship which was removed in 1859 whilst under repair following an explosion.

Sturdily built from local stone the aptly named Springhead occupies an enviable position opposite the millpond. A deeply padded chesterfield suite and daily papers on a side table create a cosy comfortable and welcoming feel as you enter the main low beamed bar. A separate dining room has seating for 55 and there are tables outside overlooking the pond with more in the large rear garden, which has a children's play area.

Jim & Julie White have managed the Springhead for the past seven years under Devenish and lately Greenhalls and have now taken the tenancy. The well stocked bar has a very good wine list and an exciting range of single malt whiskeys plus a choice of two regular real ales Flowers I.P.A. and Popes, plus a couple of guests in summer.

Very good home cooked food is available all week, the restaurant recognised as one of the best in the area. Bar bites include ploughman's, super salads, jacket potatoes and sandwiches also home-made soup, the pub's own smooth chicken liver and Cognac cream pate, crispy mushrooms, Springfield skins. Followed by their own home-made tasty meaty sausages very good home-made steak and kidney pie and Texas chilli, For those wanting something more the daily specials might be roast Barbary duck breast, lamb fillet roasted to a juicy medium rare, served with a freshly made redcurrant sauce and fresh braised rabbit. For fish lovers there could be red bream fillets or crab thermidor. Good value family Sunday lunch.

Dogs are allowed and children welcome with guardians.

Opening times 11 - 2.30 and 6 - 11. Sunday 12 noon - 3 and 7 - 10.30.

Telephone: (01305) 832117. Fax: (01305) 835210.

*"Here stretch the downs, high and breezy and green,
absolutely unchanged since those eventful days."*
The Melancholy Hussar

Biographical Notes:

Hardy's interest in the Napoleonic Wars began well before he started research-
ing material for THE TRUMPET MAJOR in 1878. Originally his interest was
stimulated by his own family oral history.

Hardy recalled that during one hot and thundery summer in his childhood, his
grandmother remarked to him "It was like this in the French Revolution I
remember". In his Memoranda notebook of October 1888, he wrote "My mother
says that my (paternal) grandmother told her she was ironing her best muslin
gown (then worn by young women at any season) when news came that the
Queen of France was beheaded. She put down her iron, and stood still, the event
so greatly affecting her mind. She remembered the pattern of the gown so well
she would recognise it in a moment."

On his honeymoon he tramped the battlefield of Waterloo with Emma, and
looked in vain for the site of the famous Duchess of Richmond's Ball, held the
night before the battle.

On 18th June 1875, on the sixtieth anniversary of Waterloo, Thomas and Emma
had visited the Chelsea Hospital to chat to the old campaigners who remembered that battle.

When the novel was published, an old man of ninety wrote to Hardy, telling him
that he had witnessed the arrival of the soldiers on Bincombe Down, just as
Hardy had described it.

The manuscript of THE TRUMPET MAJOR was presented to George V in 1911
and is now in the Royal Library at Windsor Castle.

Literary Associations:

Sutton Poyntz is one of the more difficult places to pinpoint. Overcombe is
Hardy's fictional name for the area (not to be confused with the real
Overcombe, which lies between Weymouth and Preston). The existing mill at
Sutton Poyntz was not there in Napoleonic times but is the site of the original
Lower Mill. The Upper Mill was demolished in 1856. The fictional mill resem-
bles more closely the old mill at Upwey, near Weymouth. But the mill pond is
instantly recognisable from the description of the scene from Anne Garland's
window:

"Immediately before her was the large smooth mill-pond, over-full, and intruding into the hedge and into the road. The water, with its flowing leaves and spots of froth, was stealing away, like Time, under the dark arch, to tumble over the great slimy wheel within....."

The Trumpet Major (the head trumpeter in a cavalry regiment), ostensibly the hero, does not marry the heroine, Anne Garland, who ends up with his brother, Bob the sailor. The army provides the colour and magnificence in the book with accurate descriptions of the large camp on the downs and the reviews of his troops by George III. After his inspection the downs were bare again:

"They still spread their grassy surface to the sun ...but the King and his fifteen thousand armed men, the horses, the bands of music, the princesses, the cream-coloured teams...how entirely have they all passed and gone!"

On the hillside, King George III and his White Horse, 280 feet long by 323 feet high, galloping away from Weymouth, much to the King's annoyance, were cut in the chalk by soldiers in 1808. Here John and Anne paced

"from the horse's head down his breast to his hoof, back by the way of the King's bridle-arm, past the bridge of his nose, and into his cocked hat...".

Poxwell Hall (Oxwell Hall) home of Squire Derriman, described in the book with *"muddy Quadrangle, archways, mullioned windows, cracked battlements, and weed-grown garden"*, which eventually becomes Anne Garland's property, can be seen from the Weymouth-Wareham road.

In the course of his research for THE TRUMPET MAJOR, Hardy came across the real incident concerning two German soldiers of the York Hussars who were shot for desertion on Bincombe Down: ...."*they dropped instantly, and expired without a groan. The men wheeled in sections, and marched by the bodies in slow time.*" "The Melancholy Hussar Of The German Legion" is Hardy's fictional version, later made into a film.

We are again the country of THE DYNASTS, the ultimate epic saga of Napoleonic times, reshaping the fruits of many years of research.

Historical Interest:
The White Horse with George III and a zig-zag path down the incline from the camp to the riverhead can be discerned today. The original hexagonal brick gatehouse of Poxwell was constructed in 1634. The Manor was built by the Henning family, Poole merchants.

The view from Bincombe Barrows, the area abounds in earthworks, is one of the most extensive in the country. A large camp was formed here in apprehension of invasion by Napoleon.

Bincombe Church is small and ancient, with a circular Norman font. In the Parish register the burials of the two German deserters are entered, dated June 30th 1801.

The Walk:

Village signed from the A353 at Preston.

Approximate distance: 3½ miles. OS Map 194 SY 707/838.

There are car parks to the rear, the side and at the front plus ample space beside the pond.

Hilly and a bit demanding this very scenic walk on field paths and wide gravel tracks takes you up to the top of the well known White Horse Hill. Although generally good underfoot the valley can be muddy in winter and early spring.

1. Leave the pub turning right walking until you reach the path on the right. Follow the track through a couple of gates keeping straight ahead close to the hedge. Cross the stile and continue ahead to the gate opposite maintaining direction to the pair of stiles and to a gate after which bear right, cross the stream and follow the path to the gate in the far corner, out onto the bridleway and turn left.

2. Often muddy at first the track rises steadily towards a stile and gate then fairly steeply up onto White

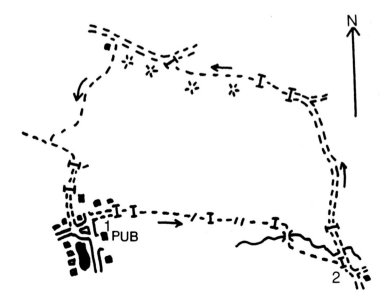

Walk No. 14

Horse Hill. After resting awhile to take in the view over Weymouth Bay continue through the gate towards Bincombe, through a second gate and then a third bearing left along the track. Just before the derelict buildings turn left and follow the track (path signposted). A short distance ahead peel left onto the narrow path leading down the hillside to a cross track then turn left. Climb the stile at the bottom keeping to the track through the gates, past the pumping station back to the pub.

The mill pond, Sutton Poyntz

King George III

SWANAGE
(Knollsea)

The Durlston Inn
Swanage

The Isle of Purbeck is a unique area of unspoilt rocky cliffs, high downs, sandy bays and ancient tracks. Purbeck marble has been used for centuries in the building of many great monuments including Durlston Castle. Built in Victorian times by George Burt today it is home to J's restaurant. The bar is at the front in the high grand entrance hall, which has a fireplace in one stone wall leading to a central tiled room with metal patio furniture. On one side there is a games room and a food servery the other. There is a small informal dining area at the rear plus an attractive restaurant in a pink and grey decor. The rear terrace overlooks the sea beyond, which is a sloping beer garden with more seating on the sunny front terrace. Theme nights are held on a regular basis

Real ales presently on offer include Theakston Old Peculier, London Pride, Ringwood Best Bitter, Courage Navigator and beers from the Quay Brewery.

Food listed on the chalkboard on my last visit included garlic bread, prawn cocktail, deep fried mushrooms with a garlic dip, home-made pate, whole prawns in garlic butter, avocado baked with prawns and cheese, prawn and cheese tortilla, mushrooms stuffed with crab and Stilton. Followed by pizza, smoked poached haddock, assorted summer salads, fresh fillet of plaice, various steaks, pork fillet in white wine sauce, chicken curry, mussels mariniere, lasagne omelettes. A small specials board also listed scallops in bacon, rack of ribs in hickory sauce, and wild mushrooms in filo. There is a children's selection plus hot sweets like spotted dick and treacle roly poly with a tempting cold selection on the trolley.

The Castle is presently open all day from 11 - 11.
Telephone: (01929) 424693.

"...*a seaside village lying snug within two headlands*
as between a finger and thumb."
THE HAND OF ETHELBERTA

Biographical Notes:
In July 1875, the Hardys travelled from Bournemouth to Swanage by steamer, where they took lodgings with a former captain of smacks and ketches, called Joseph Masters. West End Cottage still exists at the end of a cul-de-sac by Belvedere Road. It is a semi-detached cream painted building about 150 years old, bounded by the wall of Sentry Road. The first notebook of Emma's Diaries gives the West End Cottage address. Hardy wrote a poem about the fuchsias lining the path in the front garden;

> *Mrs Masters' fuchsias hung*
> *Higher and broader, and brightly swung,*
> *Bell-like, more and more*
> *Over the narrow garden-path,*
> *Giving the passer a sprinkler-bath.*

In September 1892, the Hardys returned to Swanage on a visit. Thomas attended a meeting of the Field Club whilst Emma showed the Owen sisters, American admirers of Thomas, round the town. Mrs Masters remembered her, but she declined to go inside the cottage. Emma never liked THE HAND OF ETHELBERTA - it had "too much about servants in it".

In later life, on 31 October 1919, Thomas opened the Swanage Children's Hospital, Hill Side, Peverill Road.

Literary Associations:
Hardy had already written the first chapters of THE HAND OF ETHELBERTA before going to Swanage. It is described by him as a "somewhat frivolous tale" largely set in the drawing rooms of London. Ethelberta had advanced her social status by marrying the son of her employer, who died shortly afterwards. The young widow strove to maintain her position by becoming a professional story-teller, whilst keeping secret her impoverished relations who were employed "below stairs". But to please her sister Picotee, she took rooms in Swanage for a holiday. The cottage, high on the hillside looking out over the bay and the cliffs of the Foreland, is obviously the one the Hardys lived in. Captain Masters also appears in the novel as Captain Flower. He spoke in a "rich voice, developed by shouting in high winds during twenty years' experience in the coasting trade". Later, when Ethelberta was expecting a proposal from Lord Montclere, a dis-

reputable rake, she moved to a better address to "this porticoed and balconied building" (unidentified), not without regret.

While living in Swanage, Hardy had one of his poems published, written much earlier in 1860. "The Fire At Tranter Sweatley's" was accepted by Gowing for The Gentleman's Magazine.

Historical Interest:
Swanage is famous for the Tilly Whim caves, Durleston Head and the Dancing Ledge. The old church, the mill and several stone cottages would have been there in the fictional Ethelberta's time. John Wesley once spent a night in a cottage near the church. A plaque records the event, dated August 13th 1782. Hardy was fascinated by the quarries, known for Purbeck marble, mined from the top vein, and the more abundant building stone much used in London, which was shipped out from Swanage quay.

Old Harry Rocks are still visible but "Old Harry's Wife" crashed into the sea on the same night that the lifeboat was wrecked in a gale.

The Gothic clock tower once stood on London Bridge, and the façade of the Town Hall came from Mercer's Hall, London, and was designed by Sir Christopher Wren. Built in 1774, it is said to be the smallest town hall in England.

The Great Globe, Durleston

Walk No. 15

The Walk:

From Swanage follow the signs to Durlston Country Park. Inn located in Lighthouse Road.

Approximate distance: 3 miles. OS Map 195 SZ 034/773.

Pay and display car park at top of the drive and opposite by the visitor centre.

A most enjoyable scenic walk from Durlston Head to Swanage returning through Durlston Country Park, an area of outstanding natural beauty. The 261-acre Park was created in 1973 with the help and support of both The Countryside Commission and Swanage Council. Orchids and other wild flowers abound at Durlston together with 33 species of butterflies, a dozen species of grasshoppers and over 200 species of birds.

1. From the Castle take the wide path north hugging the cliff top, which descends gently towards Swanage through very attractive woodland at one point crossing a bridge in a pretty valley. Most of the trees were planted over a century ago and include Californian cypress, holm oaks from the Mediterranean, privet and spindle from Japan and native oak, ash and beech. Viewpoints allow glimpses across the sea to the I.O.W. and Bournemouth coastline. If you look carefully you may even see the resident seal in Durlston Bay. At the top of the steps turn right and right again through the gate onto the grass. Bearing left walk down and across to the small gate in the wall. West End Cottage lies at the end of Belvedere Road opposite. A blue plaque commemorating Hardy's stay.

2. Carry on down the hill turning left into High Street. Fork left at the junction uphill past the Town Hall turning left into Chapel Lane, a narrow path that runs up beside the church entering the road at the top. Continue uphill past the hospital and take the next but one turning on the

right (footpath signed). Turn right into Rough Height, walk up the drive, past the dwelling and along the grass path ahead. Cross the tarred track, pass through the squeeze gate and

continue following the undulating path ahead.

3. Further on the path passes between a number of grass mounds before meeting a cross path at which point turn left up the hill to the squeeze gate. (take time to look behind you and enjoy the view). Cross the track and stile and continue up the field ahead to the wall and enter Durlston Country Park. Head towards the gate, climb the wall and walk around the field to the stile ahead, go over and turn left making for the small gate.

4. Paths go in all directions allowing one to roam freely but by following the path ahead you get a good view of the lighthouse. After passing the visitor centre you can return directly to the pub or take the path on the right signposted, to Tilly Whim Caves. The route leads to the lighthouse after which you can return along the lower path up past the globe. Conceived by stone merchant and owner of the castle George Burt it weighs forty tons and was carved in Greenwich from 15 pieces and assembled at Durlston.

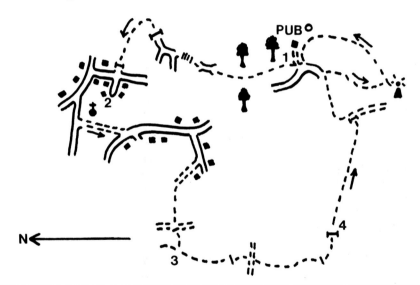

Walk No. 16

WEST BAY
(Port Bredy)
& BRIDPORT

Bridport Arms Hotel
West Bay

Seats overlook the harbour at this interesting, thatched two-story pub, which occupies an enviable position on the edge of the shingle beach. The lounge is on two levels providing comfortable areas for both drinking and dining and has old local photographs displayed on the walls above the green padded settles. The smaller locals bar has a nice flagstone floor with high back wooden settles and a large attractive fireplace. There is a family room and separate restaurant.

The pub is owned by the local Palmers Brewery serving three of their popular real ales Palmers Bridport Bitter, 200 and I.P.A.

Food is served all week from 12 noon - 2 and 7 - 9. Soup of the day is listed on the bar menu together with deep fried cheese with salad and redcurrant, herring roes on toast and hot buttered crab with granary bread also a choice of ploughman's, jacket potatoes and sandwiches. Local whole plaice and lemon sole naturally features together with trout stuffed with prawns and home-made fish pie together with meat options like home-made chilli and cottage pie. Daily specials on my visit included half a melon filled with prawns, grilled lamb chops and cold roast chicken salad. There is a separate menu for children and a vegetarian selection which presently lists hazelnut, lentil and mushroom pate, carrot and nut roast, cheese and vegetable bake and lentil patties with red pepper and garlic sauce. Additional dishes served in the restaurant range from devilled West Bay crab and sauté squid with garlic to medallions of fillet steak in a cream, brandy and green peppercorn sauce.

13 bedrooms with tea/coffee making facilities, 8 with T.V., 6 en-suite.

Opening times: summer all day Monday to Friday 11 - 11 Sunday 12 noon - 10.30. Winter Monday and Tuesday 11 - 2.30 and 6.30 - 11 otherwise as summertime.

Children in family room and play area only dogs allowed in bar.

Telephone: (01308) 422294. Fax: (01308) 425141.

*"The shepherd on the east hill could shout out
lambing intelligence to the shepherd on the west hill,
over the intervening town chimneys, without great inconvenience
to his voice, so nearly did the steep pastures encroach
on the burghers' backyards."*
                                            "Fellow Townsmen"

Biographical Notes:
John Hicks, in whose architect's office Hardy trained as a young pupil, worked
on the restoration of St Mary's Church, Bridport, in the 1860's, possibly while
Hardy was still with him.

In July 1886, Hardy invited his friend Gosse (writer and critic) to Max Gate. He
was very anxious that Gosse should see Bridport - but it was a disaster. Hardy
wrote apologising for "that terrible kettle at the Bridport pot-house" and Gosse
later related how "they then missed the train back after being elaborately mis-
directed by a local inhabitant."

Literary Associations:
Tess lives briefly at a dairy (unidentified) near Port Bredy before trudging on to
the hated Flintcomb-Ash. There is another brief mention in "The Withered
Arm" when Mr Lodge, having seen his natural son hanged, retired to Port
Bredy. But the story "Fellow Townsmen" is firmly set in Bridport and West Bay.
The two townsmen, Barnet and Downe, drive "past the little town hall, the
Black Bull Hotel and onward to the junction of a small street on the right....",
recognisable as East Street, the Bull Hotel and King Street, which is where
Downe lived. Barnet lived in East Street, where the site is occupied now by a
chapel. Downe and Lucy Savile were married in St Mary's Church opposite.
Hardy describes the rope walks in the lower lanes of the borough where Barnet
"looked at the rope-makers walking backwards, overhung by apple trees and
bushes and intruded on by cows and calves, as if trade had established itself
there at considerable inconvenience to Nature".

The short story, published in "Wessex Tales" was set in the 1840's, when
Harbour Road leading to West Bay was sparsely populated. Lucy's cottage was
near the West Bay end, possibly No.74. Chateau Ringdale, a rather grander
mansion, no longer exists, but the site is thought to be on the road now known
as Wanderwell.

Walk No. 16

West Bay, the "little haven, seemingly a beginning made by Nature herself of a perfect harbour" nevertheless does experience rough seas at times. Mrs. Downe and Mrs Barnet were capsized in their boat at West Bay, resulting in the untimely death of Mrs Downe.

Historical Interest:

In Saxon times Bridport was one of the four royal boroughs of Dorset. It is mentioned in Domesday Book, with a mint and an ecclesiastical establishment. When Henry VIII was king, it was prescribed by royal edict that all cordage used in the Royal Navy must be made in Bridport, its reputation dating back to the early 13th century. All the flax used in manufacture was grown locally. The hangman's noose also traditionally came from Bridport; being "stabbed with a Bridport dagger" became the colloquial expression for being hanged. The town still produces fishing nets, lines and cordage but artificial fibres have largely replaced hemp and flax. Wimbledon tennis nets are made in Bridport.

To the east of the town, at Lee Lane, a stone monument commemorates the escape of Charles II after the battle of Worcester.

West Bay was previously known as Bridport Harbour. At one time there was a flourishing trade with Scandinavian timber but the constant silting up of the port with shingle from Chesil beach brought it to an end. Shipbuilding, too, declined when iron boats superseded wooden ones.

The Great Western Railway extended its line to a terminus here in 1884 and renamed the place West Bay, hoping that it would become a busy holiday resort. There are tourists who visit West Bay in the summer but it retains its character as a fishing village.

The Walk:

West Bay is signed from the Bridport by-pass, the pub is on the east side of the harbour beside the shingle beach.

Approximate distance: 4¼ miles. OS Map 193 SY 463/904.

There is parking beside the wall opposite the pub, ample pay and display car parks close by, on the approach road and at the old station yard car park

An extremely enjoyable walk at first along the course of the old railway then up a pretty bridlepath onto Bothenhampton Nature Reserve. Further paths guide you to Bridport passing St Mary's Church. The return route is along a lovely path beside the River Brit.

1. Walk back to the road and turn right past the shops crossing over when you reach the old railway car park. Carry on past the station following the course of the old railway, which eventually reaches the B3157. Cross over and join the signed bridleway opposite. This very attractive primrose lined path winds its way steadily to the lane at the top. Keep straight ahead past the dwellings and through the gate onto Bothenhampton Nature Reserve. A short way in take the small path downhill on the left and either fork left over the crossing point which passes the old lime kiln or carry on ahead. Leave by the gate at the

bottom, follow the track up to the road, turn right and join the signed footpath on the left.

2. This very attractive, deeply cut, stone sided gully rises steadily to a track at which point turn left, enter the cul de sac and, keeping to the pavement on the left walk down to the road and cross to the footpath opposite signposted, Bridport ¾. Pass between the dwellings at the bottom carefully crossing the by-pass to the kissing gate opposite.

3. Keep straight ahead, cross the river and join the path behind the houses round to the gate, up the lane turning right into the road. Cross over and

walk up to St Mary's past the front entrance and take the path on the left round behind the church and join the tarred path leading to the River Brit, Go over the bridge and turn left along this very attractive riverside path. Cross the road and continue ahead on the signed footpath. Bear left past the thatched dwelling, through the kissing gate keeping to the path under the by-pass. Well signed the path bears right to a gate follows the length of the fields through a couple more gates before reaching the caravan park. Bear left along the path, up to the road back round the harbour to the pub.

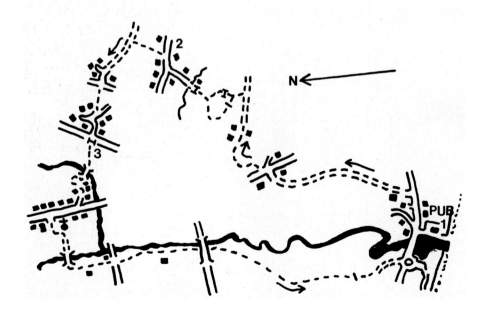

St. Mary's Church, Bridport

The harbour, West Bay

Walk No. 17

WEST
KNIGHTON &
WINTERBORNE
CAME

The New Inn
West Knighton

Originally 18th century farm cottages today the New Inn is a very popular local. The main bar, divided by a central fireplace is given over to games at one end and seating the other. There is also a good sized and comfortable dining room, separate skittle alley and rear garden with chairs, picnic benches and a children's play area.

Two well-kept real ales presently available are Ruddles County and Courage Best. From October Greenalls are taking the pub back and installing a manager. Any changes will be too late for inclusion in this edition.

The inn has a good reputation locally for very good and tasty home cooked food. Heading the specials board on my last visit was New Inn bake - chicken, bacon and sausage in a mushroom sauce topped with vegetables on a potato base with a cheesy crumble topping also spaghetti, beef Madras, poachers pie, steak and kidney pie, lasagne, tagliatelle, ham and mushroom and pork and cider with stir fry vegetables. There was a rack of spare ribs in a barbecue sauce and liver, bacon and onion casserole. Fish dishes included fresh Portland dressed crab, pink trout fillet covered in almonds and bread-crumbs, tiger prawns in filo pastry with a garlic dip, deep fried battered cod and salmon kouliabac - salmon with a vegetable terrine in brioche bread. Vegetarians could choose between wild mushrooms in brandy sauce, veg-etable curry, Brie, potato courgette and almond crumble and hot cheese tomato and onion quiche. Tempting hot sweets ranged from apple pie with custard and fruit crumble to treacle tart and Jamaican pancake with banana and coffee ice-cream. Snacks and meals on the printed menu include ploughman's, sandwiches, jacket potatoes and omelettes plus local ham, egg and fries, steaks plus a three course traditional Sunday lunch

Children welcome in dining room dogs welcome if kept under control.

Weekday opening times are from 11 - 2.30 and 7 - 11.

Overnight accommodation is available in one self-contained room.

Telephone; (01305) 852349.

WEST KNIGHTON

Biographical Notes;
In 1893, aged 53, Hardy supervised the restoration of St. Peter's Church, West Knighton. The contractor was his brother, Henry Hardy. In 1990 a beam with "Hardy" chalked on it was found in the chancel roof. Sketches of his design for the restoration of the tracery in two of the windows appear in his Architectural Notebook. Hardy is credited with persuading Dr. Hawkins of Lewell, the local squire, to fund the project.

Literary Associations:
At this time Hardy was writing JUDE THE OBSCURE and although the setting for this novel was Oxford, the builders and stonemasons working at West Knighton lent something to the character of Jude, the stonemason. In the novel Jude and Sue are called in to "undertake the relettering of the Ten Commandments in a little church". These "towered sternly over the utensils of Christian grace, as the chief ornament of the chancel end" exactly as they do at West Knighton.

Hardy's poem "The Young Glass Stainer" (November 1893) was written while he was working on the windows of the church.

Walk No. 17

Historical Interest:
Signs of prehistoric life, notably at Little Mayne, where there are the remains of an ancient stone circle, the Sarsen or Little Mayne Rocks. West Knighton, Little Mayne and Fryer Mayne are all mentioned in the Domesday Book. West Knighton was originally called Chenistetone, derived from the Anglo-Saxon, meaning "place of lesser knights". The ancient manor of Knighton became the property of the Knights Hospitaller in 1304 and remained so until the dissolution of the lesser monasteries.

WINTERBORNE CAME

Biographical Notes:
Main association is with William Barnes. Hardy met him as a young man in Dorchester. John Hicks' Architects office, where Hardy trained, was next door to William Barnes' school in South Street. From 1862-1886 Barnes was rector of St Peter's Church and is buried in the churchyard there in Winterborne Came. On many occasions Hardy walked from Max Gate to visit his grave. For many years Barnes lived at Came Rectory, a small, early 19th century thatched building (cottage orne style). Hardy and his wife Emma visited him there before and after Max Gate was built.

Literary Associations:
The sight of the sun glinting on Barnes' coffin as Hardy walked across the fields to his funeral inspired the poem "The Last Signal" (11 October 1886). In the poem he uses the internal rhymes found in Barnes' own poetry as a tribute to his old friend.

Historical Interest:
Came House (1754) is attributed to Francis Cartwright of the Blandford School, a provincial master-mason.

Winterborne Farringdon a quarter of a mile west of the church is a well preserved deserted medieval village, with the ruins of St. German's church.

The Walk:

Village signed at Broadmayne from the A352 between Dorchester and Wool.

Approximate distance 6½ miles.   OS Map 194 SY 732/876.

Park at the front or through the arch at the back. Very limited parking in the village.

Generally good underfoot this enjoyable walk both scenic and interesting throughout guides you along bridleways to Max Gate, Hardy's Dorchester home afterwhich field paths take you to Winterborne Came and the church where William Barnes is buried, before returning across farm land and bridleways passing through the village of Whitecombe.

1. Leave the pub and turn left carefully walk down and round the bend turning left onto the bridleway. After passing the farm buildings pick up the narrow grass track walking until you reach a stile on the right. Walk up the field to a similar stile opposite and take the path across to one last stile keeping straight ahead along the grass bridleway. Enter the road at

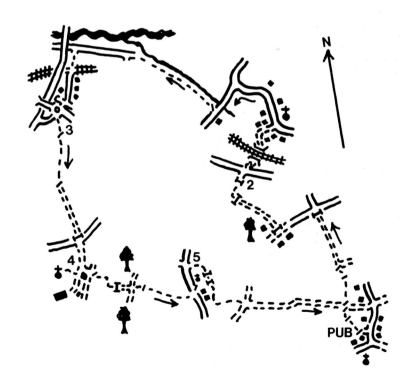

99

Sixpenny Gate and turn left towards Stafford Farm. Just beyond the main buildings go through the wide metal gate on the right, up the track beside the small bluebell wood which later dips to a gate. Turn right beside the hedge, up to the gate and out into the road.

2. Carefully cross the by-pass and join the signed bridleway opposite. Pass under the railway bridge following the track straight ahead past the dwellings and up to the road opposite the church at West Stafford. Turn left and keeping to the right-hand side follow the road round the bends walking until you reach the bridleway on the right signposted, Dorchester 2 miles. Often overgrown in summer this attractive path runs beside the river and leads to a small trading estate. Keep straight ahead and after passing the letter box but just before reaching the bridge go up the little path on the left, carefully cross the railway and keep straight ahead up the road and take the next right to the entrance of Max Gate.

3. Return to the road by the roundabout, then cross the by-pass and join the bridleway opposite signposted, Winterborne Came ¾. The path runs up the field to a gate, through a small wood and down a gravel drive to the lane. Keep straight ahead into the drive opposite. In early spring the air is filled with an intoxicating smell from the numerous garlic smelling ransoms. Keep straight ahead following the sign and the narrow path to the church.

4. Retrace your steps back along the drive to the fingerpost, along the track and over the crossing point opposite. Walk up the field ahead, bear right at the quarry, pass through

Max Gate is the house which Thomas Hardy designed and his father and brother built in 1885. He lived here until his death in 1928. Here he wrote THE WOODLANDERS in 1887, TESS Of THE D'URBERVILLES in 1891, JUDE THE OBSCURE in 1895, the WELL-BELOVED in 1897, THE DYNASTS in 1904-8 and most of his great poetry. The poem "Everything Comes" written after the death of his first wife Emma describes her feelings about the house after they first moved in and Hardy's response to her complaints. During his time here he entertained many of the most famous people of the time including Edward VIII, Lawrence of Arabia, Rudyard Kilping, H.G. Wells, R.L. Stevenson, Virginia Woolf and Gustave Holst, The house is owned by the National Trust and open from April until the end of September Monday, Wednesday and Sunday from 2 - 5.

St Peter's is best known for its association with Dorset schoolmaster, cleric and poet William Barnes who was rector at Came and the tiny church at Whitcombe. He is buried in the churchyard under a tall stone cross close to the south-west window. Came House, just visible at the top of the field is a fine example of a small Palladian country house built by the Damer family in 1754.

Max Gate

St Peter's Church, Winterborne Came

the gate into the small wood and keep straight ahead. Cross the track and bear left along the narrow path, into the field and bear left down to the gap in the far left-hand hedge. Because of mature crops I found it necessary to walk round the perimeter of the field. Upon reaching the road turn left, cross over and walk up to the church. 5. Either cross the stile, go past the church to the gate and into the field at the back or carry along the verge and join the signed footpath on the right. Cross the field to the gate, walk past the buildings and, staying close to the fence make for the gap in the hedge then turn left along the footpath. Cross the track keeping straight ahead into the field on the right and soon after climb the crossing point into the field on the left. Bearing right pass behind the pub across to the stile at the rear of the new dwellings back to the pub.

The Church of St Andrew, West Stafford

Key to Symbols

════ road	---------- track	---------- undefined path
∕ stile	⤝ bridge	⊢⊣ gate
⊣ ⊢ gap in hedge	⊟ cattle grid	

WEST STAFFORD
(Froom Everard)
STINSFORD
& BOCKHAMPTON
(Mellstock)

The Wise Man
West Stafford

This quaint thatched, 400-year-old inn is tucked on the outskirts of Dorchester in the small village of West Stafford. Accommodation comprises two bars, a comfortable and cosy lounge and a simply furnished but homely public bar heated by a warm open fire, and which features a collection of Toby jugs and cases of antique pipes collected from around the world by a previous landlord. Adding a touch of colour, Morris men can sometimes be seen in the summer dancing on the forecourt, the sight of which can be enjoyed siting at the tables in front of the pub. The contained rear beer garden offers further seating for up to 32 people in very pleasant surroundings.

David Bailey, the newly appointed landlord of this Greenalls pub, is a real ale enthusiast who serves two regular real ales, Draught Bass and Marston's Pedigree plus two guest ales.

Food is served all week except Sunday evenings in the winter. Apart from snacks like ploughman's typical blackboard specials might include a home-made turkey curry, home-made beef chassuer, steak and ale pie, fresh cod cooked in the pubs own beer batter and for vegetarians a vegetable lasagne. For the sweet toothed there are sorbets and traditional English puds like spotted dick, jam roly poly and lemon sponge. There is a roast on Sunday.

Families and dogs are equally welcome.

Weekday opening times are from 11 - 3 and 6 -11.

Telephone: (01305) 263694.

*"As they came out of church the ringers swung the bells off
their rests, and a modest peal of three notes broke forth -
that limited amount of expression having been deemed sufficient
by the church builders for the joys of such a small parish."*
TESS OF THE D'URBERVILLES

Biographical Notes:

Thomas Hardy was born at Higher Bockhampton in 1840 (Upper Mellstock).
His father ran the family firm of stonemasons from the cottage and they lived
there until 1914 when the surviving children moved to Talbothays Lodge, West
Stafford, built by Henry Hardy in the 1890's.

Hardy's first school, built by Julia Martin of Kingston Maurward 'for the education of children of the labouring classes', lies at Lower Bockhampton not far
from the bridge. Now a private residence, it can be distinguished by the school
bell hanging over the porch.

The Hardy family has long been associated with Stinsford Church. Hardy's
grandfather, father and uncle all played in the "Mellstock Quire". His mother,
Jemima, once worked at Stinsford House and met his father in Stinsford
Church, as described in the poem "A Church Romance". Hardy, in 1920, helped
with the repair of the old Norman font found in pieces in Stinsford churchyard.
He designed a new stem and base after sketching similar fonts in churches in
Martinstown and Dorchester. The Hardy family graves are in the churchyard.
When Thomas died in 1928 his ashes were buried in Poets Corner,
Westminster Abbey, but his heart is with his first wife, Emma Lavinia, in her
grave at Stinsford.

Literary Associations:

The first published novel DESPARATE REMEDIES (1871) centres on Kingston
Maurward House (Knapwater House) in the Parish of Stinsford. Hardy was
criticised for placing two fictional manor houses so close together in the book,
but at Maurward these can still be seen. The Georgian house, originally built in
brick, was the residence of Miss Aldclyffe and her young companion, Cytherea.
The older Tudor mansion was the home of the villain of the piece, Manston.
The lake and the stream are still there.

Hardy's first really popular work was UNDER THE GREENWOOD TREE cen-
tring on the Stinsford area he knew so well. He used the Bockhampton School
as Fancy Day's place, where she lived and taught. His own home at
Bockhampton is recognisable as Dick Dewy's home. The Mellstock of the novel
covers Stinsford and the Bockhamptons and various isolated houses and small
hamlets in the area.

Walk No. 18

This part of Dorset was used over and over again in Hardy's work. The Mayor of Casterbridge walked up Cuckoo Lane in search of Farfrae. Wildeve and Thomasin married in Stinsford Church (Mellstock Church) in THE RETURN OF THE NATIVE. Most famously, in TESS OF THE D'URBERVILLES, the valley of the Great Dairies, the valley of the Froom or Var (the Celtic name) is where Tess and Angel met and fell in love. (The name Angel can be seen on the Grey memorial in Stinsford Church.)

Although the name Talbothays Dairy was derived from land owned by Thomas's father, the fictional building resembles more closely Lower Lewell Farm at West Stafford. The present building called Talbothays Lodge was not built when TESS was published.

The Church of St. Andrew is the scene of Tess's marriage to Angel Clare. West Stafford House (Froom Everard House) appears in the short story "The Waiting Supper". The description "mullioned and transomed Elizabethan style" refers to the building as it was in the nineteenth century before later enlargement. Hardy describes the River Froom in all its moods. In May Tess sees the waters 'clear as the pure River of Life shown to the Evangelist' but in July thunderstorms fill the meads and flood the lane between West Stafford and Bockhampton and Angel has to carry the milkmaids across the floods to reach church.

Historical Interest:
Kingston Maurward - the old Manor House. A stone house a quarter of a mile from the new house. Hutchins refers to a shield in the hall dated 1591, possibly the year the house was completed. Over the entrance doorway, family arms record the alliance of Angel Grey with Katherine Stawell in the time of Charles I.

1747 - Lora Pitt (nee Grey) applied to Parliament to build a bridge to span the Frome at the bottom of Dorchester. Permission was granted in 1748 and she built the stone bridge known as Greys Bridge ever since. Lora married George Pitt who built the new Georgian house. Originally of brick, King George III is said to have voiced his disapproval, "Brick, Mr Pitt, Brick," and Mr Pitt at vast expense had the house encased in stone.

Stinsford House was at one time occupied by Lady Susanna Strangways, born 1743, daughter of the first Earl of Ilchester. She eloped with an actor William O'Brien. Walpole said "I cannot have believed Lady Susan could stoop so low. Even a footman were preferable". They lived at Stinsford House(now derelict) and Lady Susan ordered a vault to be made "just large enough for our two selves only". Hardy's grandfather built the vault as she wished. (See the poem "The Noble Lady's Tale") Another lady of Kingston Maurward built a bridge over the Frome at Lower Bockhampton. This was constructed by the Hardy family and

Thomas's father was presented with the Book of Common Prayer when she laid the foundation stone on July 2 1833. This was Mrs Morton Pitt.

The Walk:

West Stafford is signed from the Dorchester by-pass alternatively turn off the A35 Troy Town by-pass and take the turning signposted, to Higher & Lower Bockhampton. Keep straight ahead at the crossroads through lower Bockhampton turning left at the road junction.

Approximate distance: 5½ miles. OS Map 194 SY 726/896.

Park at the front or in the side car park.

Quite long and a little demanding this very enjoyable and interesting walk is both historical and scenic taking in the birthplace of Thomas Hardy, the area where he grew up and Stinsford church where he worshipped, and where his family, together with his own heart are now buried. Generally good underfoot the walk crosses open heath and farm land, passes through attractive woods and along peaceful tracks and country lanes; it both crosses and follows the banks of the River Frome and its tributaries, and passes through the tiny villages of Higher and Lower Bockhampton.

1. Leave the inn and follow the lane up and out of the village to the left. You will soon see the Manor House on your left. After passing a sign, which reads "concealed entrance 100 yards", turn left into the Dairy House drive and immediately go through the metal gate into the field on the right. Bearing left make your way down to the crossing point in the far hedge. Walk to the stile opposite, across the next field and over the stile onto the narrow path, which bears right into the lane.
2. Turn left along the track, pass through the gate, cross both bridges and go through the gate ahead into the field. Follow the path over the plank bridge then cross the stile into the field and turn right. In fifty paces negotiate the wooden bridge over the river and make for the metal gate opposite. Go along the wide grass track (muddy in places), leave by the far gate and turn left. Keep to the signed bridleway, across the concrete bridge and almost immediately pass through the gate into the field on the left. Keeping close to the hedge walk round and up the field to the gate then follow the track ahead, round the farm buildings and out into the road.
3. Walk straight across to the stile opposite, enter the field making for the stile in the far boundary. Cross a second stile and then bear right onto the wide path, which rises at first, dips and then heads very steeply up Durdle Heath. Bear left at the top and keep walking along this wide track for quite some distance until you eventually reach a junction of five tracks at which point

turn left. Bat boxes can be seen attached to the surrounding trees. Keep to this track which will eventually take you past the memorial stone to Hardy (erected by his American admirers) and Hardy's Cottage. The exterior is open from the 1st April until 30th October daily, except Thursday, from 11 a.m. till 5 p.m. Interior by appointment only. Continue past the cottage along the gravel road, up to the lane and turn left.

4. Soon join the bridleway on the right signposted, Kingston Maurward 1 Stinsford 1¼. Walk down to the barn at the end of the gravel track, pass through the small metal gate and continue down the field to the gate at the bottom. Follow the diversion (if in place) otherwise bear left across the field to the gate on the far side, pass through, cross to the stile on the right and take the narrow path uphill through the woodland strip and out through the gate into the road at the top.

5. Turn right, go past the entrance to Kingston Maurward College (Knapwater House) and take the next left signposted, Stinsford Church (Mellstock Church). The graves of the Hardy family are on the left as you enter the churchyard. Leave by the rear gate into the lane and follow the attractive bridleway ahead turning

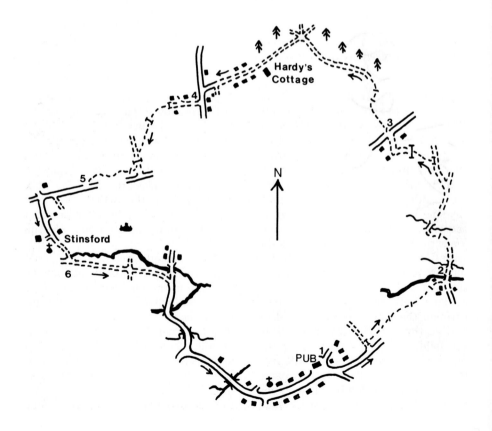

left towards Lower Bockhampton.
6. This very attractive path runs beside the stream from which you have a good view of Kingston Maurward House. Upon reaching the lane turn right then left at the road junction. Keep to the right-hand side carefully walking the half mile back to the village passing West Stafford House (Froom Everard House) and the church of St Andrew.

Hardy's birthplace

Walk No. 18

Greys Bridge, Stinsford

The Stour, Pamphill

WIMBORNE
(Warborne)
Pamphill

The Vine Inn
Pamphill

Sir John Bankes purchased Kingston Lacy in 1623-36 and in 1663-65 built a new family seat on the site of the medieval manor house. The house was lived in by successive members of the family until the late Ralph Bankes died. The estate was then bequeathed to the National Trust in 1981. Milk quotas were responsible for the closure of nearby Pamphill dairy, which now operates as a café and shops.

Throughout Dorset there are few pubs that compare with the delightful little Vine Inn. Originally part of the Bankes Estate and now owned by the National Trust the inn is set on a hillside overlooking rolling green fields in a peaceful scenic position close to the River Stour. The inn sign is one of the oldest in the country and refers to the Roman vineyards. The inn has not altered in all the years I have been coming nor I suspect has it for the locals who congregate in the tiny public bar. The lounge is marginally bigger seating up to twelve. Most people though enjoy sitting in the sunny front garden or under the grape-laden conservatory. Some even play draughts a long standing tradition.

The inn is run as a freehouse by the long standing tenants serving well conditioned real ales from the barrel which presently include Castle Eden Ale plus various guests.

Space restriction confines bar snacks to freshly prepared ploughman's and sandwiches served at lunchtimes only weekdays 11 - 2 and Sunday 12 - 2.

Children are not allowed inside but there is no objection to dogs.

Weekday opening times are from 11 - 2.30 and 7 - 11. Sunday 12 noon - 3 and 7 - 10 30.

Telephone: (01202) 882259.

How smartly the quarters of the hour march by
That the jack-o'-clock never forgets;
      Poem: Copying Architecture in an old Minster

Biographical Notes:
Hardy passed through Wimborne when he was working on the restoration of the church at Hinton Martell. Later he visited the town when searching for a suitable house to rent, when he sat in the Minster late at night, listening to the organist practising by the light of a solitary candle. Six years later the Hardy rented Lanherne, a Victorian house built in 1872. On the first night there they saw Tebbutt's comet sail overhead. They let their coach-house to a young pupil land agent, Francis John Douglas, the younger brother of Sir George Douglas, already an admirer of Hardy, who became a lifelong friend. He later supplied some young trees to shelter Max Gate.

Hardy had his hair cut at Lock's the Barber, the shop is now a jewellers in the High Street. While in Wimborne he joined The Society for the Protection of Ancient Buildings. His first action for the Society was to inspect repair work required in the Minster. He often sketched in the building. A drive around the countryside with Emma and sister Kate with a gossiping wagon driver gave him the theme, together with the glimpse of the tower at Charborough Park, of the novel about a budding astronomer TWO ON A TOWER he wrote at Wimborne. The wagon was hired from The George in the Cornmarket. Two years later the Hardys departed to fulfil their original intention of settling in Dorchester.

Literary Associations:
Several poems were inspired by his stay in Wimborne. "Copying Architecture in an old Minster", "The Levelled Churchyard" and a nostalgic remembrance sent many years later to Sir George Douglas, "they are great trees, no doubt, by now" of the young lime trees with which the Avenue was planted when he lived there.

The railway and the station (now demolished) were important to the story; and the lack of lighting at the time helped the clandestine lovers as they walked through the town on their way from the station. The Grammar School where young Swithin St. Cleeve was educated; "a place where they draw up young gam'sters brains like rhubarb under a ninepenny pan", has been converted into town houses but looks much the same externally.

The tower in Charborough Park (Welland Park) is visible from various points. Charborough House is long and low but the interior descriptions are imaginary. The candlelight scene Hardy experienced in the Minster is repeated in the book, but now it is Viviette, Lady Constantine, who sits in the church by candlelight, which is streaming over the Ten Commandments, rather significantly.

Canford Manor, now a public school, was used as the setting for Hardy's short story 'Barbara of the House of Grebe'. Hardy visited the manor with Emma and much admired the medieval architecture surviving in the kitchens known as John o' Gaunts Kitchen. But Lord and Lady Wimborne had held a shooting party on the day they dined there and the reporting of the huge 'bags' may have led to his expression of utter abhorrence of pheasant shooting in TESS OF THE D'URBERVILLES.

Historical Notes:
King Ine of the West Saxons founded a double monastery in Wimborne in about 705 A.D. for his sister Cuthberga to head as Abbess. This was destroyed by the Danes but refounded by Edward the Confessor as a Minster. The central tower once carried a spire, which collapsed during the 10 o'clock service one day in 1600, without causing any casualties.

The Minster is famous for its chained library, founded 300 years ago, and the astronomical clock of around 1320, which shows the belief of the time that the earth was the centre of the universe with the sun and moon circling it. The quarter jack on the bell tower was installed in 1612. It was then the figure of a monk. During the Napoleonic wars it was repainted as a Grenadier.

The Grammar School was founded in 1496 by the mother of Henry VII and granted a new charter by Queen Elizabeth I in 1562. The present building dates from 1851 when the school catered for boarders.

The centre of the town is much the same shape as it was in the 16th century but was enlarged in the 18th century with Georgian buildings, many of which are still to be seen in West Borough.

Walk No. 19

The Walk:

Pamphill signed off the B3082 Wimborne to Blandford road. Pub in Vine Hill just past the school.

Approximate distance: 6 miles. OS Map 195 ST 994/003.

Park anywhere along the lane by the green.

A fairly long but enjoyable walk, which follows a path beside the Stour to historic Wimborne, field paths then take you to High Hall returning along peaceful country lanes and tracks.

1. Leave the pub and walk down Vine Hill to the road junction, cross to the squeeze stile opposite, head for the river and go over the stile into the field on the left. Follow the path ahead up to another stile maintaining direction ahead. The twin towers of the Minster come into view as you enter the allotments. On the far side turn left between the cottages, go up to the road, turn right and then left into West Street. At the bend turn right into West Row, bear left then right into the Corn Market passing the entrance to the Minster.

2. Turn left into the High Street then left into the Square and right into West Borough. Walk the length of the town passing the recently restored Tivoli and Walford Mill. After passing

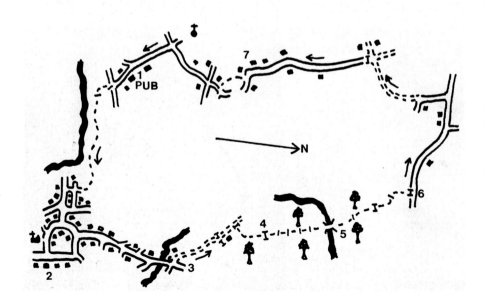

114

the Crown & Anchor and garage turn left onto the gravel track signposted, to High Hall.

3. Pass round the metal gate to the left of the waterworks and keep straight ahead along the track up to a similar gate on the right. Keeping to the wire fence walk to the top of the field, turn left and follow the track ahead beside the bluebell wood.

4. Pass round the farm gate keeping straight ahead, through the squeeze gate and across the field to the stile. Follow the boardwalk through the coppice to the stile, climb into the field and maintain direction over a couple more stiles before reaching the River Allen.

5. Cross the bridge bearing slightly left and head for the stile in the far hedge, walk through the coppice, over the stile into the field and up to the gate on the right-hand side of High Hall. Further on cross the stile into the field on the left and bear right down to the gate turning left into the lane.

6. Walk until you eventually reach a tarred road on the left leading to Lower Barnsley farm, go up to the bend and keep straight ahead onto the track. Upon reaching the entrance to Chilbridge Farm turn left through the metal gate into the lane. Several picture post card cottages make a delightful backdrop to the flower filled hedgerows in this very peaceful lane.

7. Just before the left-hand bend climb the signed bridleway on the right, turn right into the lane and carefully cross the main road into the lane opposite. Go past the old dairy (now shops and tea-rooms) and turn left opposite the church returning past the school and sports field with its attractive thatched pavilion.

Lanherne, Avenue Road, Wimborne

WOOL
Bindon Abbey
(Wellbridge Abbey)
Woolbridge Manor
(Wellbridge Manor)

The Seven Stars
East Burton

Located just outside the village of East Burton this imposing pub is set back from the lane in a raised sunny position with fields to the rear. A traditional atmosphere is maintained in the inter-connected heavily beamed and boarded bars. A central fireplace serves both a games room and the main seating area and there is a separate attractive dining room. A vine covers the pergola and terrace, beyond which is a large children's play area and animal farm.

The inn is a freehouse very well run by the owners. A good of choice of real ales include Castle Eden Ale, Ringwood's True Glory and Tetley Bitter.

All food is freshly prepared and cooked to order maybe creating delays at busy times. The usual snacks of ploughman's, sandwiches and jacket potatoes are available together with giant pizzas. The menu supplemented with daily specials such as king scallops cooked with onions, mushrooms and peppers, flamed with Pernod and finished with cream, lists home-made soup and snails in garlic butter followed by a 16 ounce trout stuffed with celery, apples and walnuts, fillet of lamb Seven Stars - strips of lamb pan fried with garlic, onions and mushroom in a coriander, lemon and pepper sauce and tropical fillet of chicken sauté with onions, mushrooms, pineapple and peppers in a cream sauce flamed with a banana liqueur. Chef's tempting home-made specials range from seafood lasagne to Hawaiian pork - diced with onion, pineapple, peppers, garlic, tomatoes and herbs. There is a separate children's menu and at least 6 vegetarian dishes such as pan fried vegetables in oyster sauce served in a filo pastry basket and stuffed peppers with rice, onions, mushrooms, tomatoes, broccoli, peas and sweet corn.

Weekday opening times presently 11 - 2.30 and 6 (6.30 winter) - 11 Sunday 12 - 3 and 6 (winter 6.30) -10 30

Children welcome but not dogs.

Telephone: (01929) 462292.

*"...once portion of a fine manorial residence, and the
property and seat of a d'Urberville, but since its partial
demolition a farm-house."*
TESS OF THE D'URBERVILLES.

Literary Associations:
In the valley of the Great Dairies, the Manor is famous for the scene in TESS
OF THE D'URBERVILLES where Angel Clare and Tess spent their honeymoon. Angel Clare confessed to his wife that he had once "plunged into eight-
and-forty hours' dissipation with a stranger." Tess was relieved that Angel had
committed such an indiscretion because she realised that he had not received
the note in which she told him about Alec d'Urberville and the subsequent birth
of a child that died. But while Tess could forgive Angel, he was appalled by her
confession. "O Tess, forgiveness does not apply to the case. You were one person;
now you are another". They slept apart and decided to separate. On the third
night of their estrangement Angel, sleep-walking, rolls her in a sheet "as in a
shroud" and carries her to Wellbridge Abbey where he lays her in an empty
stone coffin. For the purposes of the story, the abbey is portrayed as being much
nearer the Manor than is actually the case.

On arrival at the Manor, Tess was startled by life-size portraits on the wall of
two women with "their long pointed features, narrow eyes, and smirk of the one,
so suggestive of merciless treachery; the bill-hook nose, large teeth, and bold
eye of the other, suggesting arrogance to the point of ferocity." "Those horrid
women" .... "How they frightened me". The portraits exist, much faded, of
Julia Turberville on the left, and Frances Tuberville on the right.

Historical Interest:
Like Wool Bridge, the Manor is Elizabethan in origin, although the front of the
Manor was re-built in 1652, probably as a consequence of the Civil War. It was a
possession of the Turberville family. Bindon Abbey (Wellbridge Abbey) lies half
a mile east of Wool station. Founded for Cistercian monks in 1172, it was
granted to Thomas Lord Poynings at the dissolution of the monasteries and sold
to the Weld family of Lulworth afterwards. Legend has it that the 12 bells of the
Abbey were stolen in the night and now grace the churches of Wool, Combe and
Fordington. Hence the jingle:

*"Wool streams and Combe wells
Fordington cuckolds stole Bindon Bells."*

The Manor, Wool Bridge

Bindon Abbey

The Abbey ruins and deep fishponds remain and the empty stone coffin can be seen.

The Manor has a legend to tell about the Tuberville coach, which passes over the bridge and draws up at the old house on Christmas Eve. The sounds are audible only to certain ears and foretell death or calamity.

The Walk:

Pub in East Burton Road, East Burton signposted ¾ mile from the A352 opposite the garage and just before the level crossing.

Approximate distance: 4½ miles. OS map 194 SY 811/858.

Ample parking at pub plus limited space in the front lane.

An easy walk for the most part along peaceful country lanes and field paths guiding you through Giddy Green and Wool to Bindon Abbey returning past Woolbridge Manor and twice crossing the Frome.

1. Turn left out of the pub then next right towards Giddy Green, go over the railway crossing and at the bend turn left into Giddy Green Road signposted, to Wool. Walk to the end of the cul-de-sac and join the small footpath beside the drive. Cross the field and road keeping to the narrow lane out to the main road and straight across into Colliers Lane.
2. Follow the path through the estate, past all the dwellings and out into Lulworth Road turning left and then right into Spring Street. Cross the bridge on the right into Church Lane walking round past the church and up to the farm gate. Cross the stile into the field and bear left making for two stiles in the far bottom corner. Walk the width of the field to the bridge ahead, over a second and bear right across an often-damp area of field to the bridge in the hedge, go out

into the lane opposite Bindon Abbey and turn left.
3. Walk round and up to the road junction turning right into Station Road then right again over the level crossing. Cross the road after the garage where there is a Hardy information board and left across bridge passing the Manor on your left.
4. At the top of the lane keep to the footpath on your left, turning left further on into Bovington Lane. In just under a mile (after passing the entrance to the tank museum worth a visit if you have the time) go up the short drive on the left and climb the stile onto the footpath signposted, to East Burton.
5. This narrow undulating path winds through a small wood and follows the edge of a field before meeting a stile. Cross the track to the stile

opposite and walk through the wood to the bridge. A series of bridges allow easy access across the low-lying fields and the Frome itself. After a final bridge turn right following the track, up past the cottages turning right at the junction back to the pub.

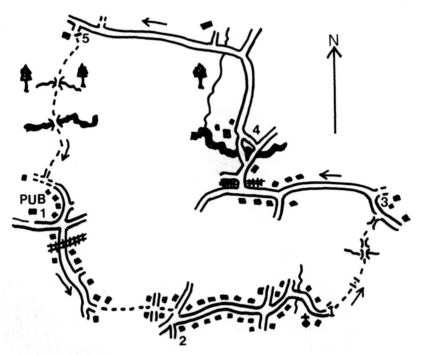

The Church at Wool